The Price of Punishment:
Public Spending for
Corrections in New York

Other Titles in This Series

Westview Special Studies in Contemporary Social Issues

The Price of Punishment:
Public Spending for Corrections in New York

A Report of The Correctional Association of New York
and the Citizens' Inquiry on Parole and Criminal Justice, Inc.

Douglas McDonald

Despite the intensity of the national debate concerning control and correctional policies, neither the costs of existing agencies nor of alternative approaches are adequately understood. Accurate figures are not reported to private citizens or public officials, and spending is fragmented among different agencies and governing units. This study presents a comprehensive description and analysis of how much money was actually spent in New York in 1977-1978, at all levels of government, for each of the control systems that incarcerate or supervise criminal offenders/defendants. After a broad overview of criminal justice spending, it details spending for prisons, jails, probation, and parole; evaluates the services provided by these public expenditures; and discusses proposals for alternative penal policies and their fiscal implications. The book concludes with recommendations for improved government cost accounting, as well as suggestions for broader penal reforms. Although restricted to an analysis of New York, the findings and recommendations are broadly relevant to other regions of the country.

Douglas McDonald, a sociologist, is director of the Citizens' Inquiry on Parole and Criminal Justice, Inc. The Correctional Association of New York and the Citizens' Inquiry are private organizations with a longstanding involvement with criminal justice reform.

The Joint Report of
The Correctional Association of New York
and the Citizens' Inquiry on Parole
and Criminal Justice, Inc.

The Price of Punishment: Public Spending for Corrections in New York

Douglas McDonald

with the assistance of
Betty J. Bernstein

Westview Press / Boulder, Colorado

Westview Special Studies in Contemporary Social Issues

Published in 1980 in the United States of America by
     Westview Press, Inc.
     5500 Central Avenue
     Boulder, Colorado 80301
     Frederick A. Praeger

Library of Congress Catalog Card Number: 80-80512
ISBN: 0-89158-912-0

Composition for this book was provided by the author.
Printed and bound in the United States of America.

JOINT COMMITTEE
FOR THE
CRIMINAL JUSTICE COSTS PROJECT

Ramsey Clark
    Clark, Wulf, Levine & Peratis
    Chairman, Citizens' Inquiry on Parole
    and Criminal Justice
George G. Walker
    Chairman, The Correctional Association
    of New York
Betty J. Bernstein
    Co-Director, Criminal Justice Costs
    Project
Diana R. Gordon
    Vice President, National Council on
    Crime and Delinquency
Douglas McDonald
    Director, Citizens' Inquiry on Parole
    and Criminal Justice
Adam F. McQuillan
    Former President, The Correctional
    Association of New York
Dan Pochoda
    President, The Correctional Association
    of New York
Susan A. Powers
    Special Assistant Attorney General with
    the Special Prosecutor for Nursing
    Homes, Health, and Social Services
David Rudenstine
    Associate Professor of Law, Cardozo Law
    School

STAFF FOR THE
CRIMINAL JUSTICE COSTS PROJECT

Douglas McDonald   Betty J. Bernstein, Ph.D.

Part-Time Staff

Martin Barr   Doreen Reel

Mira Kyzyk   Sally Silvers

Cathy Zall   Marna Walsh

Contents

ix

x

Tables and Figures

Figures

Acknowledgments

This report has benefited from the contributions of
many people and organizations. Most important were
the hundreds of public officials who patiently an-
swered our queries, read and corrected preliminary
drafts of the various chapters, and directed us to
other sources of data. Many went far beyond the
call of duty in their help and we regret that they
are too numerous to be thanked individually. Most
crucial was the cooperation of the agencies examined
in this report. Their executive officers and employees gave us an enormous amount of fiscal information. We especially appreciate the cooperation of
the New York State Department of Correctional Services, the State Division of Parole, the State Division of Probation, the State Department of Audit and
Control, the State Commission of Correction, the Division of the Budget, the New York City Departments
of Correction and Probation, the City Office of Management and Budget, the Office of the New York City
Deputy Mayor for Criminal Justice, and the New York
City Office of the Comptroller. We also thank the
county executives and legislative committees in
Westchester, Rockland, and Rensselaer counties, as
well as corrections and probation officials there.

George Walker conceived of the project and
proposed the collaboration between the two sponsoring organizations. Other members of the Joint Project Committee spent long hours reading successive
drafts of this report and attending numerous meetings. Their patience and guidance are very much
appreciated. Dan Pochoda's contribution is especially large. Although he came to the committee
after the project was underway, he had a strong hand
in shaping the final product.

Very helpful were the criticisms, suggestions,
and advice of Marsha Garrison, Richard McGahey,

xv

Karen Reixach, and David Beier. To the latter I
owe a special debt for his long hours of stimulating
discussion and patient reading of earlier drafts. I
am also indebted to John Taylor for editing the
final draft.

Betty Bernstein's contribution to this report
has been enormous. She established the general approach to be made in the fiscal analysis and collected a good portion of the fiscal information.
After the research had begun she turned her efforts
to writing the companion volume to this report entitled *Calculating Criminal Justice Costs: A Manual for
Citizens*. At all stages of the project she remained
a valuable source of advice, direction, and intelligence.

Martin Barr provided much assistance in writing
Chapters 5 and 6. New York City's jail costs were
among the most difficult to estimate, and Marty's
resourcefulness and ingenuity were considerable.
Chapter 6 draws very heavily upon his earlier
drafts.

The job of typing what seemed to be endless
drafts fell upon Doreen Reel and Marna Walsh. Marna
singlehandedly produced the final copy of the manu-
script, an arduous and tedious task. I am grateful
for her innumerable last minute editorial suggestions and especially for her patience.

Finally, financial support for this project was
provided by generous grants from the North Shore
Unitarian Veatch Program, the Mary Reynolds Babcock
Foundation, the Chemical Bank, and several anonymous
donors. Without their public-spirited contributions
this publication would not have been done.

Douglas McDonald

Introduction

Crime and punishment have always been matters of vital interest, but the character of public concern has taken a rather special turn in recent years. Confidence in the ability of our corrections system to "correct" has withered. The belief that the criminal justice system can effectively control crime has been sharply challenged in many scholarly studies. Criminal sentencing policies have been scrutinized more intensely in the past few years than at any other time in this century and wholesale revisions have been enacted in a number of states.

Despite the waning of confidence in the criminal justice system, record numbers of people are being brought under some form of custody for criminal charges. More than 1.5 million American adults were in prisons and jails, or were under supervision by probation and parole officers, on any given day during 1978.[1] Reliance upon the most expensive penal sanction of all, imprisonment, is increasing at a quickening pace. By the end of 1978 the proportion of our nation's adults in prison reached an all-time high.[2] Prison construction is a booming industry.

The cost of this expansion is dimly understood, which is especially surprising given the intense concern shown recently for other types of government spending. Throughout the country citizens are closely scrutinizing government budgets and are demanding to be shown real returns for their taxes. Although determining the "benefits" of a particular expenditure for criminal justice and corrections is extraordinarily difficult, it is nevertheless remarkable that costs have been so poorly explored. To be sure, some broad social costs of a particular criminal justice program resist accurate estimation. These include, for example, increased support for families of jailed breadwinners, the prisoners' re-

xvii

duced contribution to the GNP, and the like. But
even those most elemental costs, expenditures by
public agencies for criminal justice, remain pecu-
liarly invisible.

This invisibility is largely due to inadequate
reporting and accounting. For example, one corrections agency in New York which spends over $100 mil-
lion a year has not issued an annual report in over
a decade. Even when available, reports frequently
give an incomplete picture because many of the costs
that they ought to record are charged to other government accounts. For example, the high cost of employee benefits is paid in many cases not by the individual agencies, but instead is buried in the
"miscellaneous" section of the general government
budgets. In New York City the Department of Correction budget reflected no more than 64 percent of the
total jail cost during fiscal 1978. Similarly, the
budget of the State Department of Correctional Services accounted for only 77 percent of the total
prison costs that year. No single agency integrates
either the administration or fiscal reporting of
criminal justice operations throughout the state.
Rather, this criminal justice "system" is a crazy
quilt of more than 3,000 public agencies working at
various levels of government, each with its own
budget.

New York is not alone in its inadequate public
accounting practices. One study by the First National Bank of Boston and Touche Ross & Co., an international accounting and consulting firm, found
that the books in half of the 120 American cities
they investigated were so badly kept that they could
not be audited.[3] Another study by the Council on
Municipal Performance found that only twelve states
in the country enforce uniform or widely accepted
accounting standards for their underlying jurisdictions.[4] In short, the accounts in most states do not
readily reveal how much money taxpayers spend on
criminal justice and corrections.

To help private citizens and public officials
understand these costs and thereby make more intelligent choices in the issues of crime and punishment, the Citizens' Inquiry on Parole and Criminal
Justice, Inc., and The Correctional Association of
New York have jointly produced this report. Its
primary focus is on the cost of the postconviction
stages of New York's adult criminal justice system:
prison, parole, jails, and probation. This focus
was chosen because of the great amount of money involved and because the public debate about criminal

sentencing has intensified in recent years.

Expenditure information was examined for criminal justice and corrections agencies operated by the state government, by New York City, and by three counties: Westchester, Rockland, and Rensselaer. These counties differ in the extent to which they are rural or urban, in the size of their tax bases, and in the makeup of their corrections systems. Although they are not representative of all other counties in the state, they are illustrative of spending at the local level.

To identify all corrections-related costs, visits were made to three state prisons, and to jails in New York City and Rockland, Westchester and Rensselaer counties. Meetings and conversations were held with hundreds of public officials who supplied expenditure and budget data, descriptions of how monies were spent, and assisted in developing estimates where the existing information was incomplete.

The information collected in the course of the research was augmented by the expertise and information previously accumulated by both sponsoring organizations. The Correctional Association of New York, founded in 1844, has long been active in criminal justice reform. It is the only citizens' organization with legislative authority to enter prisons and jails, and its findings and recommendations are reported to the legislature. It was instrumental in introducing indeterminate sentencing practices to New York. It developed probation and parole services, which were then assumed by state and local governments, and inaugurated the campaign to establish an independent State Commission of Correction to oversee the penal facilities in the state. The Correctional Association proposed and helped draft legislation establishing the Crime Victims Compensation Board; it operated the first program of free civil legal services to detained prisoners; and it was instrumental in prompting Governor Carey to establish a commission to review current sentencing practices in the state.

The Citizens' Inquiry on Parole and Criminal Justice, Inc. was formed in the wake of the Attica uprising in 1971 to examine New York's penal system. In 1975 it published a report on parole which stimulated widespread debate about current parole and sentencing procedures. This was followed by an active public education effort which included workshops with judges, parole board members, prisoners, legislators, and members of the general public. It proposed a model parole system; published a bimonthly bulletin; and prepared a handbook on parole for prisoners and the lay public. It has since expanded its range of concerns to include research on probation and sentencing practices in New York State.

The Joint Committee, comprising members of both organizations, brings together a broad background of experience in criminal justice matters. Committee members have previously held a variety of positions in all levels of government, in prison and jail administration, in government budget bureaus, in agencies overseeing corrections departments, in criminal defense, and in private industry.

The Price of Punishment: Public Spending for Corrections in New York

1
An Overview of Corrections and Criminal Justice Costs in New York

New York corrections agencies -- prisons, penitentiaries, jails, probation and parole systems -- are
integral parts of a much larger network of criminal
justice organizations dispersed throughout the
state. Decisions made in these other criminal justice agencies affect how much is spent for corrections in a variety of ways. The cost of local jailing, for example, is determined in large part by police arrest practices and the bail policies of the
local courts. Because the following chapters frequently refer to the links between corrections costs
and spending for other criminal justice agencies,
this section sketches out the larger context within
which corrections must be understood.

Spending for Criminal Justice in New York

During fiscal 1977-78,* the annual cost of operating
the New York network of state and local corrections
efforts was approximately $600 million.[1] In addi-
tion, taxpayers spent an estimated $2.2 billion[2] for

---

*The accounting periods at the three levels of gov-
ernment under study do not coincide and no attempt
was made to fit all expenditures into a single time
frame. Unless otherwise noted, New York City's expenditures refer to fiscal year ending June 30,
1978, New York State's to fiscal year ending March
31, 1978, and county government expenditures to
calendar year 1977.

other criminal justice components in the state, the
most prominent of which are the police, courts,
prosecutors, and attorneys for the indigent.*

This expenditure of $2.8 billion supported a
significant portion of the total government work
force. During 1976 (the most recent year for which
employment information is available) more than
115,000 persons were on the public payroll in criminal justice agencies in New York State. This constituted about 17 percent of the total work force at
all levels of government that year.[3]

Criminal justice monies are spent in a fragmented and haphazard fashion. What is generously called
a "system" is better described as a collection of
more than 3,000 weakly coordinated public criminal
justice agencies within state borders.[4] (There are
also thousands of private organizations and individuals, but this report makes no attempt to determine how much they spend for criminal justice purposes.) No single agency administers or even monitors the spending of these thousands of dispersed
public efforts. Fiscal information about them is
therefore very difficult to obtain.

The fragmentation of the criminal justice effort
is compounded by the proliferation of different governments responsible for spending. Alongside the
state government in New York are the ruling bodies
of 57 counties (the 5 counties in New York City have
combined to form a single metropolitan government),
62 cities, 930 towns, and 556 villages.[5] Many of
these 1,600 local governments support and operate
criminal justice and corrections agencies.

Local governments shoulder the heaviest burden
of criminal justice spending. During fiscal 1977-78
only a small part (approximately 18 percent) of the
total $2.8 billion expenditure for all criminal jus-
tice operations was spent by divisions of the state
government. The New York City government spent approximately 42 percent, or about $1.187 billion.
The other local governments in the state spent the
remaining 40 percent, or approximately $1.114 bil-
lion.[6]

These expenditures represent a sizeable portion
of the entire budget at each level of government.
Although the total expenditures for all levels of

---

*Throughout this report all costs refer only to ex-
penditures for *operations* unless otherwise noted.
Capital spending is excluded because of the difficulties in amortizing these costs.

Figure 1.1

Public Expenditures for Criminal Justice
in New York, FY 1977-1978

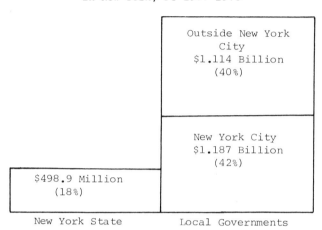

	Outside New York City $1.114 Billion (40%)
	New York City $1.187 Billion (42%)
$498.9 Million (18%)	
New York State	Local Governments

government (state and local) during fiscal 1977-78
has not been officially reported, one unpublished
source puts it at about $30 billion, of which an es-
timated $26.8 billion was for current operations;
the remainder was for capital and debt service.[7]
Criminal justice expenses accounted for about 10.5
percent of the entire spending at all levels.

New York City and other local governments allocated about 10 percent of total operating expenses
to criminal justice.[8] The state government spent
proportionately more, about 15 percent of total
spending for criminal justice.[9]

A precise description of how public monies were
divided between the various criminal justice services is impossible given the absence of adequate information. Some agencies do not distinguish civil
expenses from criminal. Moreover, information on
many types of local agencies (public defenders, police lockups, prosecutors' offices, etc.) is simply
not collected. Nonetheless, Table 1.1 shows how
some of the identifiable criminal justice costs were
apportioned in fiscal 1977-78.

About 58 percent of the criminal justice dollar
was spent on the "front line" of the criminal jus-

TABLE 1.1
How $2.8 Billion Was Spent for Criminal Justice
by All Levels of Government in New York, FY 1977-78

	Estimated Expenditure (in $ Millions)[a]	Percent[b]
Police and Other Law Enforcement	$1,624	58
State Prisons	285.5	10
Local Jails and Penitentiaries	240	9
Courts	101	4
Probation	63-78	2-3
Parole	21	0.8
Miscellaneous Other Criminal Justice (Prosecutors, Indigent Defense, etc.)	450-465	16-17
	$2,800	100%

Sources: The estimate for state and local police/law enforcement expenditures was extrapolated from 1976 distribution of
criminal justice direct and intergovernmental spending, estimated by U.S. Bureau of Census/Law Enforcement Assistance Administration, *Expenditure and Employment Data for the Criminal
Justice System 1976*, U.S. Government Printing Office (Washington, D.C., 1978), Table 6. For other estimates, see Tables
1.2 and 1.3.

[a]Expenditures by New York State and New York City refer to
FY 1978; all other local government expenditures refer to
calendar year 1977.
[b]Percentages do not add up to 100% due to rounding of figures.

tice system: the police and other law enforcement officials. Another 10 percent went to support the state prison system, 9 percent for the local jails and penitentiaries (including the New York City Department of Correction), and 2 to 3 percent for the probation departments at the city, county, and state government levels. Court costs for criminal matters amounted to an estimated 4 percent of all government spending on criminal justice.

The Specialized Responsibilities
of Each Level of Government

The governments within New York State -- municipal, county, and state -- do not spend their criminal justice dollars in the same manner. Rather, there is a division of responsibility.

Figure 1.2 compares spending on criminal justice by three different levels of government: New York City, New York State, and a composite of three county governments. Tables 1.2, 1.3, and 1.4 show the dollar amounts spent by these governments.*

Since it was impossible to aggregate expenditures for all counties outside New York City, three counties -- Rockland, Westchester, and Rensselaer -- were selected for examination. Expenditures in these three were averaged and the composite appears in Figure 1.2. These counties were chosen because they differ in a number of important ways, including size, degree of urbanization, per capita income of residents, and the complexity of their corrections systems.

---

*New York City is not representative of all city governments because it combines municipal with county responsibilities; it is used here for illustrative purposes, however, because its spending for criminal justice was the largest of any governing unit in the state.

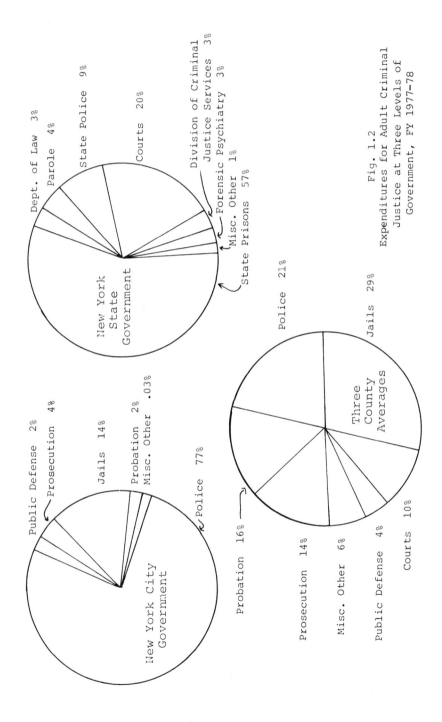

Dept. of Law 3%

Parole 4%

State Police 9%

Courts 20%

Division of Criminal Justice Services 3%

Forensic Psychiatry 3%

Misc. Other 1%

State Prisons 57%

New York State Government

Public Defense 2%

Prosecution 4%

Jails 14%

Probation 2%

Misc. Other .03%

Police 77%

New York City Government

Police 21%

Jails 29%

Three County Averages

Probation 16%

Prosecution 14%

Misc. Other 6%

Public Defense 4%

Courts 10%

Fig. 1.2
Expenditures for Adult Criminal
Justice at Three Levels of
Government, FY 1977-78

TABLE 1.2
New York State Government Estimated Expenditures
for Adult Criminal Justice,[a] FY 1978

Courts[b]	$101,433,008	20%
Commission of Correction[c]	1,709,296	0.3
State Prisons[d]	285,490,483	57
Department of Law[e]	14,440,551	3
Division of Criminal Justice Services[f]	15,403,749	3
Forensic Psychiatry[g]	16,808,090	3
Parole[h]	21,203,400	4
Division of Probation[i]	2,629,794	0.5
State Police[j]	44,329,714	9
	$503,448,085	100%

[a]Includes general fund expenditures from all public revenue
sources. Excluded are the costs of capital and debt service,
government overhead (governor's office, Division of the Budget, legislature, etc.).
[b]The Office of Court Administration roughly estimated spending
for criminal court matters only; excluded are civil court
costs and spending for overall administration. Letter 7/28/78.
[c]Computed from data given by NYS Division of the Budget, personal communication 9/21/78. Estimated fringe and pension
costs added.
[d]See Chapter 2.
[e]Not all department activities are criminal justice related,
and costs could only be roughly estimated. Spending for the
Organized Crime Task Force, NYC Special Prosecutor for the
Criminal Justice System, and a portion of general staff work
devoted to criminal justice was estimated by Dept. of Law,
letter 7/5/78 and subsequent conversations. Cost of Nursing
Home Industry Investigation estimated using data in NYS *Executive Budget*, FY 1979, p. 344. Fringe benefit and pension contributions not estimated.
[f]Includes only regular expenditures of state purposes funds.
Excludes first instance appropriations and expenditures/trans-
fers of federal funds. Comptroller of the State of New York,
Annual Report, 1978, Part II, p. 24.
[g] Accurate estimates of NYS Dept. of Mental Health spending
for criminal justice are difficult to develop. These rough
estimates were provided by Dept. of Mental Health, telephone
conversations 10/5 and 10/6/78.
[h]See Chapter 3.
[i]See Chapter 4. Excludes $19.3 million transferred to local
governments as state aid, considered herein as a local expenditure.
[j]Cost of criminal justice activities estimated from data provided by State Police, letter 10/23/78 and telephone calls of
8/11 and 8/16/78 and 9/18/78.

TABLE 1.3

New York City Government Estimated Expenditures
for Adult Criminal Justice,[a] FY 1978

Police[b]	$917,140,309	77%
Jails[c]	171,177,587	14
Board of Correction[d]	313,986	0.03
Department of Probation[e]	23,912,259	2
District Attorneys[f]	45,701,200	3.9
Legal Aid[g]	23,406,238	2
Criminal Justice Coordinating Council[h]	1,000,000	0.08
Criminal Justice Agency[i]	3,500,000	0.3
Deputy Mayor for Criminal Justice[j]	375,746	0.03
	$1,186,517,325	100%

[a]Includes general fund expenditures from all public revenue sources; capital and debt service expenditures excluded as well as some general governmental overhead costs. The city's contribution to court costs has been omitted because the Office of Court Administration was unable to segregate the amount spent for New York City's criminal courts. For total estimated cost of courts statewide, see Table 1.2.

[b]*Annual Report of the Comptroller of the City of New York for Fiscal Year 1978.*

[c]See Chapter 6.

[d]*Annual Report of the Comptroller....*

[e]See Chapter 4.

[f]*Annual Report of the Comptroller....*; estimated fringe and pension costs added.

[g]Legal Aid Society, letter of October 16, 1978; excludes spending for civil matters.

[h]Rough estimate of administrative costs only, given by Criminal Justice Coordinating Council, personal communication, November 15, 1978. Excludes all transfers of federal grant monies, which are counted here as expenditures by other criminal justice agencies.

[i]Estimated by Criminal Justice Agency, personal communication, November 27, 1978.

[j]Computed from data provided by Office of New York City Mayor, personal communication, November 16, 1978. Estimated fringe and pension costs added.

TABLE 1.4
Estimated Adult Criminal Justice Expenditures
in Three Selected New York Counties, 1977
($ thousands)

	Rensselaer		Rockland		Westchester	
	Amount	%	Amount	%	Amount	%
Police	477	14	1,368	24	6,668	22
Criminal Courts[a]	131	4	442	8	3,423	11
Prosecution	260	8	837	15	4,376	14
Defense	130	4	337	6	1,139	4
Jails[b]	824	24	1,133	20	9,472	31
Probation	836	25	851	15	4,457	15
Other	746	22	675	12	962	3
	3,404	100%	5,643	100%	30,497	100%

Sources: County Annual Reports

[a]Estimated cost of adult criminal court parts only
[b]Excludes amount identified as juvenile corrections

The Municipalities

The heaviest criminal justice cost to the municipal
governments is police. During fiscal 1978 New York
City spent 77 percent of its total funds for criminal justice operations on the police department.
In other municipalities the propotion is even higher (approximately 83 percent in 1976).[10]

The Counties

The county governments pay a large share of the bill
for processing arrest cases through the courts.
This burden includes the cost of public defenders,
court-appointed attorneys, and other programs for
assisting the indigent in their defense. Counties
also foot the bill for prosecutors' offices, for the
jails holding defendants before trial, for background investigations by the probation departments
of convicted persons awaiting sentencing by the
courts, and part of the court costs as well. (Court
costs have traditionally been a heavy county expense, but in 1976 the legislature mandated the
gradual assumption of both county and city courts by

the state government. This takeover will be completed by fiscal 1980-81.[11])

Counties also pay the cost of keeping convicted
persons who are sentenced to jail terms of a year or
less. Most of these convicts serve their time in
the county jails, although four counties have separate penitentiaries for sentenced prisoners. (See
Chapter 5.) Persons sentenced to probation are also
supervised by county departments; New York City has
a municipal department, however, and the departments
of three small upstate counties are run directly by
the state government. Most probation funding comes
from the county governments (or the municipal government in New York City), and the state reimburses
the local departments for approximately 25 to 35
percent of total costs. (See Chapter 4.)

The State Government

The state assumes the expense of incarcerating persons who have received sentences longer than a year.
This is the largest criminal justice expense at this
level of government, approximately 57 percent of the
criminal justice dollar in fiscal 1977-78. The second largest expense was the courts, an outlay which
is gradually growing, as noted above.

The cost of supervising prisoners released on
parole is borne by the state government. Some other, more general, overhead expenditures are also
paid by the state. These include an estimated $14.4
million spent by the Department of Law in handling
the legal affairs of criminal justice agencies, and
$15.4 million by the Division of Criminal Justice
Services to provide assorted services to other agencies at the state and local levels.

There are a number of other general government
costs attributable to the criminal justice efforts
of the state government -- including the cost of the
legislative and executive activities -- but these
could not be determined.

The division of state and local responsibility
for primary criminal justice expenditures is illus-
trated in Figure 1.3. Whereas Figure 1.2 shows the
spending by state, one city, and three selected
counties, Figure 1.3 aggregates *all* state, county,
and municipal spending throughout the state for fiscal 1976. (More recent data are not available for
several categories of costs. Since 1975-76, the
state share of court costs has increased. The
state/local proportion of the other costs has not
changed dramatically since then.)

Figure 1.3

The Proportion of State and Local Government Spending for Each Criminal Justice Domain: FY 1976[12]

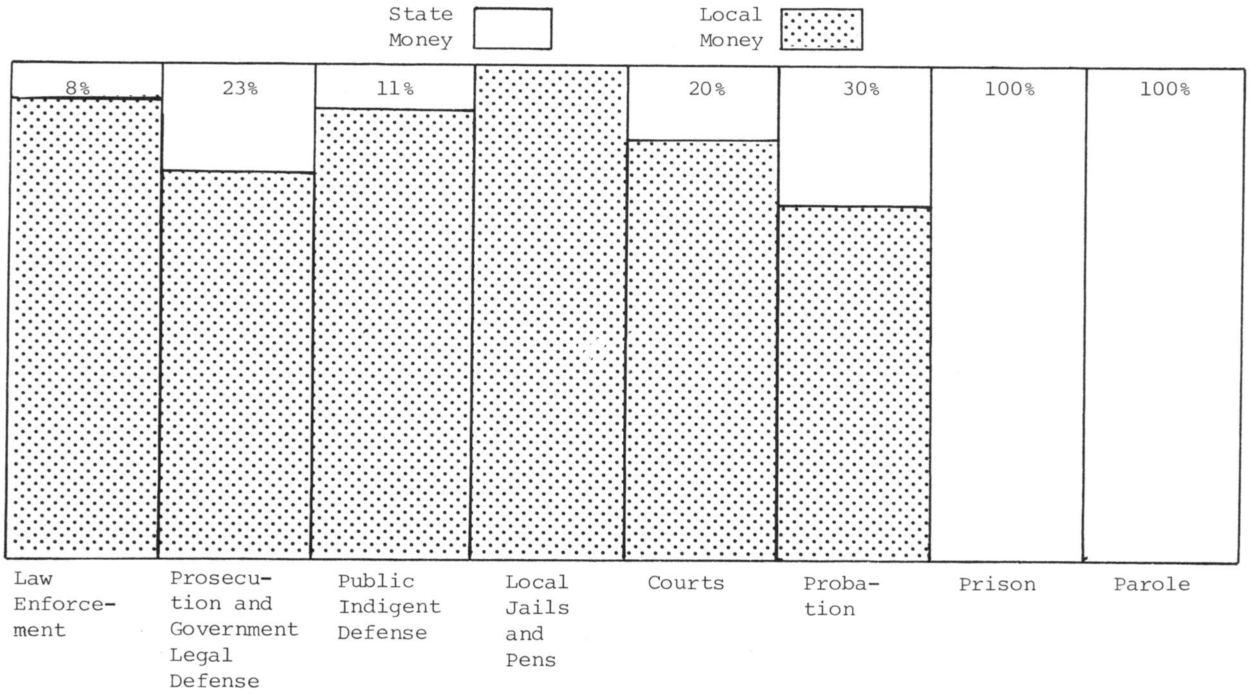

2
The New York State Prison System

Imprisonment is the most expensive criminal sanction in New York. Felons who are sentenced to terms longer than a year are sent to the state prison system, which has been growing at a faster rate during the past half-decade than at any other period in history. During the fiscal year ending March 31, 1978, the taxpayers paid a steep bill for this network of prisons: $285.5 million, or an average of $15,050 annually for each prisoner. This is simply the cost of operations and does not include the enormous expense of building prisons. State prison costs represented about fifty-seven percent of total spending for criminal justice operations by the state government during that fiscal year.

Despite the high cost of imprisonment, New York courts are sending greater numbers of convicted felons to state prisons for longer periods of time. With 20,500 prisoners* on October 15, 1978, the New York prison system has become the second largest in the nation and it promises to grow even more rapidly in the near future if current sentencing trends continue. During fiscal 1978 thirty-three state prisons employed 12,000 persons and over 28,000 convicted prisoners passed through their gates.[2] They range from huge maximum-security institutions like Auburn and Attica to small rural camps and urban "temporary release" facilities. Plans are now on the drawing boards for expanding the state system even more, at a cost of $55,000 to $70,000 per bed.

---

*During fiscal 1977-78 the average daily population was 18,968.[1] This includes those who are out to court and on work release. Throughout this report, per capita cost estimates are based on this average.

The cost of financing this expansion could drive the ultimate expense as high as $200,000 per bed.[5]

Prisons have been expected not only to securely isolate lawbreakers from the public, but also to "correct" or "rehabilitate" them so that they live within the law when released. How corrections administrators balance these demands can be determined by examining the way public funds are spent in prisons.

This chapter begins with a description of the prisoners and their needs. It then

- reviews the expenditures for prisons, examining how they reveal funding priorities for different types of services (security, basic prisoner necessities, industries, and "rehabilitation" programs for prisoners);
- explores the widely varying cost of the different facilities; and
- reviews the plans for expanding the prison system in the coming years, with a discussion of the probable costs.

Characteristics of the State Prison Population

Most of those sent to prison in New York come from ethnic minorities, are unlettered, unskilled, unemployed, and frequently have serious drug dependency problems. Fifty-five percent are black, 20 percent are hispanic, and 25 percent are white. Two-thirds had not graduated from high school before being sent to prison.[3] One survey of those sentenced to state prison in 1973 established that 68 percent were unskilled at any marketable task at time of arrest, and 18 percent were semiskilled. Fifty-six percent were unemployed when they committed their crimes. Thirty-one percent had temporary jobs, and only 13 percent were permanently employed.[4] Frequently aggravating this distressing condition were drug addiction problems. Of those in state custody during July 1977, 11,400 or approximately 60 percent of the total, were determined to be narcotics addicts at time of arrest.[5] This constellation of difficulties is also associated with recidivism: 57 percent had previously served time in state, federal, or local correctional facilities.[6] As Senator Ralph J. Marino noted, "Since the largest number of inmates...were incar-

to an estimated $60.2 million, or about 21 percent
of the total spending for prisons.* Federal grant
monies amounting to $4.7 million were also spent;
the State Department of Mental Hygiene (now Mental
Health) spent another $1.5 million for psychiatric
services in prisons; and Reality House, Inc. (private organization) spent an estimated $75,000 on
drug therapy programs for state prisoners. These
therapy programs were paid by grants from the State
Office of Drug Abuse Services (now Division of Substance Abuse) and the National Institute of Drug
Abuse.**
    Most of the money spent for prison operations
goes to employees' salaries. During fiscal 1978
about four-fifths of total operating expenses went
for salaries, fringe benefits, and contributions to
the employee pension funds. The remaining fifth
went for supplies, foodstuffs, uniforms, raw materials for industry, and the like.

The Cost of Incarceration
in Different State Prisons

The cost of keeping a single prisoner for a year varied widely from one institution to another during
fiscal 1978. The least expensive prison spent
$9,539 per prisoner, and the most expensive spent a
staggering $39,018. These differences generally
correspond to degree of security, but this correspondence runs in a surprising direction. Although
one might expect maximum-security institutions to be

---

*For every dollar paid out in salary, an average of
23.6 cents was paid into a pension fund, and another
12.7 cents was spent on additional fringe benefits.
These two added 36.3 cents to every salary dollar.[12]

**Still more money was spent for prisons that year,
but the amount could not be determined accurately
for lack of adequate fiscal information. Both public and private organizations and individuals undoubtedly spent money for prisoner education, tui-
tion assistance, legal services, and other such contributions. Moreover, the fringe and retirement
contributions of the Department of Mental Hygiene
psychiatric staff could not be assessed from the
available data.

TABLE 2.2
State Prison Facilities: Security Level, Size of Inmate Population, and Inmate-Year Costs

	Security Level	Year Opened/ Constructed	Average Pop. FY 1977-78	Inmate-Year Cost
Group I				
Attica	Max.	1931	1,762	$10,749
Auburn	Max.	1817	1,605	9,539
Clinton	Max.	1845	2,496	12,118
Great Meadow	Max.	1911	1,496	10,879
Green Haven	Max.	1941	1,870	10,382
Elmira	Max.	1876	1,570	10,860
Group II				
Ossining	Max.	1825	997	15,436
Eastern	Max.	1900	743	15,920
Fishkill	Max.	1892	1,012	20,446
Wallkill	Med.	1932	501	12,779
Coxsackie	Med.	1935	707	13,163
Woodbourne	Med.	1932	655	15,426
Albion	Med.	1893	295	17,718
Arthur Kill	Med.	1976	641	17,857
Queensboro	Med.	1976	288	17,610
Taconic	Med.	1973	184	17,522
Mid-Orange[a]	Med.	1977	161	39,018
Otisville[a]	Med.	1977	214	30,758
Hudson[a]	Med.	1976	118	27,225
Bedford Hills (female)	Max.	1901	430	20,779

Camps				
Pharsalia	Min.	1956	88	11,248
Monterey	Min.	1958	91	11,665
Summit	Min.	1961	108	11,480
Georgetown	Min.	1961	102	10,655
Adirondack	Min.	1972	187	12,365
Mt. McGregor[a]	Min.	1976	141	20,012
Community Facilities				
Rochester	Min.	1973	32	10,771
Bayview	Min.	1974	103	19,675
Fulton	Min.	1976	80	23,990
Edgecombe	Min.	1974	134	13,563
Parkside	Min.	1974	28	11,918
Lincoln	Min.	1976	88	17,918
Bushwick[a]	Min.	1976	33	34,372

Sources: Costs include state government funds spent by Department of Correctional Services and fringe benefits/pension (36.3% of personal service costs), computed from data provided by Department of Correctional Services, letter of May 7, 1979. Excludes expenditures from capital, federal, and Reality House funds. Also excluded are the costs of the department's central headquarters. Opening and construction dates from miscellaneous documents.

[a]These facilities used for only part of year.

more expensive than those labeled medium- or minimum security, the reverse is generally the case. This finding is largely explained by the way different prisons are staffed, and by the extreme emphasis placed on security in all facilities, regardless of their designated security grade.

For the sake of analysis, we have divided the thirty-three New York State prisons into five general classes: Group I and Group II prisons, camps, temporary release facilities, and the women's maximum-security prison. (See Table 2.2.) The men's maximum- and medium-security prisons were classified as either Group I or Group II on the basis of their costs and staffing patterns, to be examined below.*

Group I prisons are those six maximum-security institutions for men which held 57 percent of the total state prisoner population in fiscal 1978. These older and larger prisons were the least expensive to operate, ranging between $9,539 and $12,118 per prisoner annually, with an average of $10,856.

Group II prisons, thirteen in number, held 34 percent of the state prisoners in fiscal 1978. The annual per prisoner costs ranged from $13,163 to $39,018, but the cost of the three most expensive institutions was artificially high in fiscal 1978 because of some special start-up costs. Excluding these three institutions, the average annual cost per prisoner for this group of prisons was $16,386.

Less expensive than the second group of prisons are six prison camps which housed only 4 percent of the prisoner population during fiscal 1978. These minimum-security camps cost an average per prisoner of $11,614 (excluding the cost of Mt. McGregor, which was higher during this period due to having high start-up costs).

More expensive are the seven minimum-security "temporary release" facilities which were operating in urban centers -- primarily New York City. These house prisoners on work and education release, a program which began in the early 1970s but has since been curtailed drastically by the legislature. During fiscal 1978 only 3 percent of the prisoner

---

*Ossining, Fishkill, and Eastern resemble the medium-security prisons in their costs and staffing arrangement, despite being labeled maximum-security prisons.

population was housed in these seven facilities, at
an average annual cost of $17,244 per prisoner.
Several facilities have since been closed.

Classified separately because of its unique
character is Bedford Hills, the only state prison
for women. The average census during fiscal 1978
was only 413 women, 2 percent of the total prisoner
population in the state system. The annual cost of
keeping them there was high: $20,779 per prison-
er.

Staffing and Security

Because approximately 80 percent of the prison system operating costs is consumed by staff salaries
and benefits, the cost of imprisonment is proportionate to staffing patterns. Table 2.3 summarizes
some of these differences for the five groups of
prisons.

By comparing the two columns at the left of the
table, we see that there is a consistent relationship between the average annual cost per prisoner
and the size of the staff, measured by the ratio of
prisoners to staff. For example, in the two least
expensive types of prisons, Group I and the minimum-
security camps, there were over two inmates for
every staff person. At Bedford Hills, there were
almost as many staff persons as prisoners, and in
the community-based facilities there were *more* staff
than prisoners. As a consequence, these latter two
groups were approximately twice as expensive as the
former two, largely because there were proportionately twice as many employees to pay.[13]

The heavy emphasis on security throughout the
prison system is apparent in a comparison of the
four different types of employees shown in Table
2.3. Almost all prisons have a high ratio of security officers to prisoners, whereas there is much
greater variation in how other staff persons are employed. Moreover, the ratio of officers to prisoners *increases* as one moves from the maximum-security
prisons to the predominately medium-security prisons
(Group II), and finally to the minimum-security
temporary release facilities. The exception to this
general pattern are the six prison camps, which are
labeled minimum-security and have the greatest number of prisoners per officer.

This curious staffing pattern is a result of
departmental concern for control and preventing escapes in the less-than-maximum-security prisons. In

TABLE 2.3
Staffing Patterns of New York State Prisons, FY 1978

	Average per Prisoner Annual Cost	Average # of Prisoners per Staff	Average # of Inmates for Each Type of Staff Person			
			Security	Administration and Support	Program	Industry
Group I	$10,856	2.2	3.5	14.3	13.4	79.2
Camps	11,614	2.3	6.0	7.5	22.8	0
Group II	16,386	1.5	2.5	7.0	9.3	199.2
Community Facilities	17,244	.9	2.1	2.5	3.5	0
Bedford	20,779	1.1	2.1	3.7	7.6	103.2

Source: Staffing data from New York State Executive Budget 1978-1979.

Staff Types

Security: corrections officers and their uniformed superiors.
Administration and Support: all those who manage the basic operations of the prison, including maintenance, clerical, fiscal and personnel management and the like.
Program: psychologists, social workers, teachers, religious counselors and program coordinators.
Industry: those who manage the industrial shops in ten of the state's prisons.

the maximum-security institution much of the officers' work is done by high concrete walls, gun towers, and steel bars. Many of the designated medium-security prisons were originally built as juvenile training schools and drug treatment centers,
and are seen as needing more officers because they
are considered less physically secure.

The department's overriding concern for security in the so-called medium- and even minimum-
security facilities persists despite the fact that
prisoners are admitted to these institutions only
after a screening process and a finding that they
are not violent or serious risks. Indeed, this
concern tends to undermine the basic goal of these
lesser-security institutions -- to prepare prisoners for a return to the community by exposing them
to a less controlled and adversarial environment
than exists in the large maximum-security prisons.

Even the community-based temporary release facilities are characterized by heavy security staffing. When these institutions were opened in urban
neighborhoods, many citizens actively opposed
bringing prisoners into their communities. The department increased the numbers of security staff to
allay community anxiety and to ensure the success
of the program. Further, during fiscal 1978 the
temporary release program was shrinking. Staff lay-
offs or reassignments did not take place at the same
rate as the number of prisoner participants declined, leaving a heavier balance of staff to
prisoners.

Community-based temporary release facilities
need not be more expensive than maximum-security
fortresses. It is likely that if a network of these
minimum-security facilities were established and
stabilized, the operating costs would decline. (The
Rochester facility kept a reasonably stable population during this period and its per capita costs are
among the lowest in the entire prison system.)
Moreover, construction costs, which have been omitted here, are much higher for maximum-security
prisons.[14] One great advantage of the smaller, ur-
ban-based, minimum-security prison is that its plant
does not constitute an irreversible investment. By
contrast, once maximum-security prisons are built,
they cannot be converted easily to other uses. A
network of community-based facilities could expand
and contract more responsively to the rise and fall
of prisoner populations.

What Money Spent for Prisons Buys

Legislators, judges, criminal justice professionals, and the public ask prisons to do many different things. Prisons are generally expected to punish, not necessarily by corporal means but rather by the mere deprivation of liberty. The public also asks that prisons remove offenders from society in order to protect property, life, and limb. It is hoped however, that prisons isolate in a humane fashion without undue hardship. It has also been thought that prisons should "rehabilitate" offenders.

What prison administrators consider most important is quite easily determined by looking at how they spend their allocated public monies. The Department of Correctional Services justifies its budget requests by sorting out its various activities into four categories of general purpose: supervision of prisoners, administration/support, rehabilitation (changed to "program services" in fiscal 1979), and industries. Odd labels were devised to clothe activities in the garb of rehabilitation. For example, prisoner wages were christened "incentive allowances" in fiscal 1978 accounts. A variety of other expenditures was also described as rehabilitative without benefit of a euphemistic label. These included costs of inmate correspondence, commissary discounts, cash to outgoing prisoners, special housing (i.e., disciplinary and medical segregation units), and prisoner grievance committees.

To provide a more illuminating look at New York State prison costs, each of the specific expense items has been reclassified more descriptively. These reclassifications do not include fringe benefit and pension costs, however, for the data available did not enable us to compute this amount.[15] It is not known how these additional costs are distributed, but it is unlikely that the proportionate distribution varies greatly from the percentages shown in Table 2.4.

Whatever people may want the prison to do, it is clear from Table 2.4 that one purpose currently reigns supreme: the secure custody of prisoners. Of the $15,050 spent to hold one prisoner for one year, half of that was spent on guards. Another 22 percent was spent on general administration, plant operations, and processing prisoners in and out. Fifteen percent of the costs were for meeting basic inmate necessities, including medical services, recreation, wages, and other essentials. This means

TABLE 2.4

New York State Prison System Expenditures by Function, FY 1978
(operating expenses only)

Security	$111,458,323	(50%)
Administration, Plant Operations and Prisoner Processing	49,206,719	(22%)
Prisoner Necessities	34,033,629	(15%)
Programs	22,128,781	(10%)
Industry	13,998,134	(2%)
Other	555,069	(0.3%)
	$221,380,655	(100%)
Estimated Fringe Benefits and Retirement Fund Contributions for Department of Correctional Services Employees	60,326,732	
	$281,707,387[a]	

Source: Expenditure items for tables 2.4 through 2.15 computed from information obtained from Department of Correctional Services tables and letter dated July 19, 1978 unless otherwise noted.

[a]Does not correspond to Table 2.1 total because different data base was used. Table 2.4 was computed from expenditure reports made after the closing of the fiscal year. To these were added expenditures from federal and other department funds (except for fringe and pension costs, as noted above). Several months later, the total expenditure was reported to be $3.8 million higher, and Table 2.1 was revised to reflect this more accurate cost. The data needed to distribute this additional $3.8 million to each of the functional categories in Table 2.4 were not available, however.

that *about 87 percent of the prison system operating costs, or about $13,094 per prisoner per year, is incurred for nothing more than keeping the prisoner in custody and under guard.*

Two percent of the expenditures for the New York prison system was spent on manufacturing industries inside the walls. Prison administrators see this work opportunity as providing rehabilitative opportunities, but this claim requires closer scrutiny. During fiscal 1978 the prison industries spent more than they earned, despite the low wages paid to prisoners; this will be further discussed below.

The remaining 10 percent was spent on a variety of programs which aim to provide prisoners opportunities for self-improvement, including counseling of various sorts, academic and vocational training, and a program of temporary release (furloughs, work and educational release during the day).

In sum: security is the "bottom line" on top of which all other costs must be added. Prison administrators can lose their jobs if a single inmate escapes, but their employment is not jeopardized by a failure to provide successful programs.

Security and the Cost of Guarding Prisoners

The quasi-military correction officer force is the backbone of the prison system. Sixty-two percent of the Department of Correctional Services employees worked as uniformed officers.[16] Their salaries consumed 98 percent of the expenditure for security. [17] Table 2.5 shows how security costs are distributed.[18]

TABLE 2.5
Cost of Security (exclusive of fringe and pension costs)

Guarding prisoners	$109,918,691
Emergency Response Teams	39,681
Uniform Allowance	1,403,479
Identification	94,375
Miscellaneous	2,097
	$111,458,323

Correction officers are assigned to any location in prison where employees or other outsiders come in contact with prisoners. This includes not

only the living areas but also every other area inside and directly outside the walls. They are
posted outside to monitor the work gangs, at the
gates, and on the gun towers on the walls. Any time
inmates congregate in large numbers, such as in the
mess hall or in the yard, officers are present in
large numbers and are closely supervised by their
senior commanders. Officers accompany each of the
civilians working in the various shops and class-
rooms. Although the work in most of the shops is
coordinated by civilians (plumbers, electricians,
bakers, cooks, tailors, teachers), the correction
officers have ultimate responsibility for control.
Only officers can take an inmate into custody.

During 1978 correction officers were paid between $12,580 and $24,221, not including benefits
or overtime. (See Table 2.6.)

TABLE 2.6
Salary Ranges for Uniformed Prison Staff (as of April 1, 1978)

Title	From	To
Captain	$21,025	$24,221
Lieutenant	17,469	21,645
Sergeant	14,877	18,513
Correction Officer	12,580	15,754

There is some indication that security costs
are so high because officers are doing jobs which
could be done less expensively by civilians. An audit of security practices released by the State
Comptroller's Office asserted that during 1976 uniformed officers were needlessly employed in positions requiring no prisoner contact.[19] The audit
recommended that these officers be replaced by less
expensive clerical personnel.

The auditors also recommended that distinctions
be made between those posts requiring extensive prisoner contact, and hence greater risk, and those
which do not (e.g., positions on gun towers and outside gates). These recommendations were strenuous-
ly challenged by the correctional officers' union,
which objected to any downgrading of assignments.
Spokesmen argued that gun towers were critical posts
not only because they kept prisoners from getting
out but also kept organized outsiders from breaking

in.[20] A more important fact (left unspoken) is that
such a downgrading of the wall posts would also undermine the "career ladder" in job assignments. Officers are allowed to bid for posts, which are assigned on the basis of seniority. Many of the
older guards prefer getting as far away from inmate
contact as possible, and these wall and gate posts
are considered "plums." The unfortunate consequence
of this practice is that the younger and less experienced guards are left to work with the inmates.
This may increase the risk of riot and confronta-
tion, especially in the prisons used as training
grounds for new recruits.

Administration, Plant Operations and
Prisoner Processing Costs

Slightly more than $49 million was spent for admi-
nistration, plant operations, and prisoner admission
and discharge activities. This amounted to about
22 percent of the total cost of imprisonment. Table
2.7 details these expenditures.

TABLE 2.7
Overhead and Prisoner Processing Costs
(excluding fringe and pension costs)

Administration		
Central Headquarters	$ 7,755,368	
Facility Administration	15,599,490	$23,354,858
Plant Operation		
Housekeeping	932,849	
Plant Operation/Maintenance	20,146,989	
Auto & Truck Operation	1,731,617	
Farm and/or Grounds	1,473,268	
Fire and Safety	111,483	24,396,206
Processing Activities		
Cash to Outgoing Inmates	291,604	
Release Wear Clothing	405,090	
Inter-prison Transfers	613,863	
Transfers from County Jails	123,712	
Miscellaneous	21,385	1,455,655
		$49,206,719

Most of the central administration expenses
were paid for with state government funds, although
$525,000 came from the Law Enforcement Assistance
Administration (LEAA). Half of that amount was
spent to develop the corrections piece of the larger computerized information system which will link
all principal criminal justice agencies in the
state. The remainder was spent on legal staff, a
community relations office and staff, planning projects, library, and the development of a policy
and procedures manual. [21]
The decentralized character of prison administration is evident from the fact that about two-
thirds of the administrative expenses are incurred
at the local prison level. However, the organization of management control has changed dramatically
in recent years. Until the 1970s prisons remained
plantation-like in character. Wardens held almost
absolute control over their local domains, lived
free of charge in large houses on manicured prison
grounds, and had a number of personal servants and
cooks (all prisoners). In the mid-1970s central
headquarters sought to move prison administration
away from the feudal style and more toward the model of the corporation. Superintendents (wardens)
lost their free housing and servant privileges, and
have become more like middle-management executives,
traveling from one post to another in the statewide
system.

The Cost of Basic Prisoner Necessities

During fiscal 1978 a total of $3.4 million, or 15
percent of total expenditures, was spent to provide
prisoners with various necessities. These included
food, medical services, recreational opportunities,
nominal wages for prisoners' work, and a number of
miscellaneous other expenditures. Table 2.8 shows
these costs in greater detail.

   Food: Very little was spent on food during fiscal 1978; the annual cost per prisoner was $666, or
$1.83 per day.* Meals were not only inexpensive but

---

*This does not include the cost of cooks' salaries.
Food costs are reduced in many facilities by the use
of products grown on adjacent prison farms. Prisoners also supplement their diets with food purchased
from the commissary with their own money (savings of
their daily wages described below) or food sent them
from the outside by friends and families.

30

TABLE 2.8
The Cost of Prisoner Necessities
(excluding fringe and pension costs)

Food Preparation and Service		$12,638,535
Health Services		
Medical Services	9,803,975	
Central Pharmacy	11,908	
Admissions Exam	283,073	10,098,956
Recreation		21,113,188
Prisoner Wages		3,231,743
Miscellaneous Other		
Laundry	488,627	
Institutional Clothing	2,178,268	
Linen and Bedding	542,035	
Cell Furnishings	78,339	
Commissary	833,690	
Correspondence Unit	615,342	
Inmate Personal Hygiene	632,806	
Visiting	582,100	5,951,207
		$34,033,629

also of low nutritional quality. Menu planning in the facilities is guided by the New York State Department of Mental Hygiene Diet Manual (1974) and a Department of Correctional Services Daily Food Plan Nutrition Analysis. These two guides establish the number of pounds of food, calories, and nutritional content proposed for each inmate every day. There are no nutritionists on the staff of the Department of Correctional Services, and the chief nutritionist position in the State Department of Health (which has responsibility for nutrition in all state institutions) had been vacant for a year prior to this project's research visits. There was consequently no professional nutritionist planning the meals for the nearly 20,000 inmates in prison.

Health Services: High quality health care in prisons is especially important because prisoners have such a limited ability to treat themselves. They cannot go to a corner drugstore to purchase common over-the-counter preparations, and they cannot take the day off and stay in bed without getting special permission. Instead, they must rely on the prison health care system for all their medical needs.

Prisoners have been shown to have more medical problems than similarly aged populations in free society. Before coming to prison many were impoverished and had not received adequate medical attention. A project in San Francisco County jails in the early 1970s showed that 83 percent of the jail population had had a serious medical problem within the previous three years; two-thirds had been hospitalized within the previous five years.[22] Results from a New York County jail screening program showed that 23 percent of the prisoners required immediate medical attention.[23] Susceptibility to disease is also increased by overcrowded conditions, and the difficulties in regulating heat, ventilation, fresh air, and exercise in institutions.

During fiscal 1978 the department spent $532 per prisoner per year for medical care. This does not include the cost of transporting inmates to and from hospitals or of continuously guarding them while outside the prison. If these costs, plus fringe and pension were included, the total cost of medical services would undoubtedly be doubled. (See Table 2.9 for the total spending on medical and health services.)

TABLE 2.9
Cost of Health Services
(excluding fringe and pension costs)

Medical Services	$ 9,803,975
Central Pharmacy	11,908
Admissions Exams	283,073
	$10,098,956

Basic services at each prison include the
availability of physician and nurse care at all
times. Specialized services are available on an
irregular basis, and referrals are made to outside
resources when needed. Services in New York City
work and educational release facilities and in correctional camps are provided by private physicians
and hospitals in the area.

Providing adequate care is aggravated by problems unique to the prison health care system. The
Commission of Correction (a "watchdog" agency appointed by the governor) and the department agree
that among the major problems are the difficulties
"in recruiting and retaining qualified licensed physicians and allied health care staff due to the lack
of financial incentive, the morale problems due to
the restriction of a security environment and inmate litigation." Moreover, "the location of most
state facilities in 'physician poor' geographical
areas makes recruitment particularly difficult."[24]
Other problems include long waiting lists for outside consultative services, and the lack of definition of the levels of care required by inmates and
lack of facilities to provide services.[25]

Evaluating the quality of medical care in prison is frustrated by the absence of adequate standards. New York State has not promulgated minimum
standards for operating prison health services.
There are no system-wide evaluations or inspec-
tions, no state laws (or department regulations
having the effect of law) outlining the responsibilities of the department in health care delivery.

The Department of Health audits prison health
services only at the request of the Department of
Correctional Services. At present, only one prison is subjected to a regular medical audit.[26]

Although Correction Law requires the State Commission of Correction to oversee health care in the state,[27] the commission's performance has been sorely inadequate. The commission's Medical Review Board (created in 1975) is responsible for evaluating and inspecting the health delivery service, responding to inmate complaints, investigating inmate deaths, and assisting in developing minimum health care standards. In December 1978 the State Comptroller's Office issued an audit of the commission's performance. This audit found the commission's investigation and review of health services unacceptably deficient. The commission had not acted on a draft proposing minimum health care standards fourteen months after its submission. Only two on-site evaluations of state health facilities had been conducted. The commission's response to inmate complaints and formal grievances was improperly managed; it took an average of 258 days to close nineteen inmate grievances submitted on appeal and an average of eight months to close nineteen randomly selected cases received directly by the commission from the 286 cases closed in 1977.[28] As the commission is the only agency outside of the Department of Correctional Services with the power to implement change and evaluate prison health procedures, the audit recommended that the commission organize itself in order to be more effective in carrying out its mandate.

In the absence of effective regulation by agencies of state government, inmate litigation has forced the courts to step in and define what treatment is necessary and proper. An important class action suit in New York State radically changed the way health care was delivered at Bedford Hills. [29] The federal courts determined that "existing medical treatment procedures resulted in interminable delays and outright denials of medical care" in violation of the Eighth Amendment prohibition of "cruel and unusual punishment." No complaint was found with the staff or physical facilities, but deficiencies in screening, record-keeping, and follow-up were so great that inmates were effectively denied treatment. For example, in screening complaints, the nurses spent an average of fifteen to twenty seconds with each prisoner. There was no system of priorities in dealing with requests for medical treatment. Delays of two weeks to two months were not uncommon before seeing a physician. Inadequate monitoring procedures in the sick wing resulted in "grave and unnecessary risks" to patients. An antiquated and dangerous x-ray machine was in use. Follow-up procedures in treatment were delayed or not implemented, and results of diagnostic testing were not reported because of poor record-keeping. The complaints were so specific and well-documented that the court found the system constitutionally inadequate and ordered the department to make specific institutional changes. The results of this case are legally applicable only to Bedford Hills, but plaintiffs' lawyers feel that every other New York State prison is vulnerable to a similar suit.[30]

The issue of standards is an important one. As District Court Judge Robert Ward pointed out in *Todaro v. Ward*: "It concerns the Court that to date no one has taken the responsibility to audit the system and to evaluate its ability to deliver care to those in need. The Court suspects that the one and only thorough review of the delivery system occurred only as a result of this law suit."[31]

Prisoner Wages: Nominal wages are paid to all prisoners. Wages for those in school or work in prison jobs range from 25¢ to $1.15 per day; compensation for work in industries is somewhat higher (see below). These funds are placed in inmate accounts and are used to purchase goods from the commissary or authorized items through the mails. In earlier years prisoners did not receive wages for their work and tended to resort to gambling and "loan sharking" to raise enough "currency" (generally cigarettes) to purchase desired goods and services on the inmate black market. By receiving small allowances, prisoners can purchase their cigarettes and can more easily avoid indebtedness to other prisoners as well as the risk of violence that debts frequently entail.

Miscellaneous Necessities: During fiscal 1978 nearly $29 per prisoner was spent annually on linen and bedding, approximately $4 per cell for furnishings (chair and locker), and $74 for clothing each of the 29,337 prisoners who passed through the prisons that year. Nineteen dollars per prisoner was spent on toilet supplies and other personal hygiene items. Another $32 per prisoner was spent inspecting mail and lists of approved correspondents.

Programs Helping Prisoners to Improve Themselves: Prisoners are a handicapped population, and they need a variety of special remedial programs to help them overcome the burdens of poor literacy, lack of

trade skills, and drug addiction. Because this
constellation of drawbacks is strongly associated
with criminal behavior, prisons should be designed
so that time spent in them can be passed produc-
tively, giving the prisoner the opportunity to build
new personal skills.

The New York State prison system spent about
$22.1 million, or about 10 percent of its total ex-
penditure, for programs aimed at assisting prisoners. (See Table 2.10.)

The Department of Correctional Services classified a wide variety of activities as "rehabilitative" in nature, as noted above. In fiscal 1979
these were labelled "program services." Again, we
have reclassified some of these expenditures because
some must be considered basic prisoner necessities
or security-related costs.

TABLE 2.10
Cost of Prisoner Programs
(excluding fringe and pension costs)

Program Coordination	$ 5,364,648
Psycho-Therapeutic Counseling and Treatment	1,866,635
Drug Addiction Therapy	75,000
Academic Education	6,653,419
Vocational Education	5,295,095
Religious Counseling and Services	1,344,850
Temporary Release	1,438,596
Miscellaneous Other	90,538
	$22,128,781

Program Coordination: In the wake of the Attica
rebellion the state prison system created positions
for guidance counselors to help prisoners coordi-
nate their "treatment" programs. Civilians rather
than uniformed officers were hired for the jobs,
and these counselors act as the liaison between the
prison programs and the inmates. They respond to

inmates' requests for transfers to another prison,
for a change of cell, a new job assignment, a
change of school schedule, an emergency phone call
to home, an addition to his or her list of permitted visitors, etc. These coordinators are meant
to act as brokers of the various prison services and
not as therapeutic counselors.

Prisons also became more open to outside volunteers after the Attica uprising. To arrange these
volunteer programs, Volunteer Services Coordinators
were established in the prisons to act as liaisons
between the prison administration and prisoners and
outside volunteers. These activities cost $362,282
in fiscal 1978.

During fiscal 1978 a total of $5.3 million was
spent on the various program coordinators, or about
$283 annually for each inmates. This represented
approximately 3 percent of the total cost of imprisonment that year. (See Table 2.11.)

TABLE 2.11
Cost of Program Coordination
(excluding fringe and pension costs)

Guidance Administration	$ 193,401
Guidance Services	4,808,965
Volunteer Services Coordination	362,282
	$5,364,648

Psychotherapeutic Counseling and Treatment: This category encompasses a number of therapeutic programs
listed in Table 2.12. During fiscal 1978 approximately $98 per prisoner year was spent on these
programs.

The heaviest cost -- $1.5 million -- is spent
directly by the New York State Department of Mental
Hygiene (recently renamed the Office for Mental
Health).[32] This $1.5 million pays the salaries and
costs of psychologists and psychiatrists working
inside the prison walls, primarily seeing prisoners
in office counseling sessions. In seven prisons
there are special psychiatric units which have a

TABLE 2.12
Psycho-Therapeutic Counseling and Treatment

Psychiatric and Psychological	$ 145,103
Diagnostic and Treatment	41,043
Behavior Modification	99
Merle Cooper Therapy Program	135,237
Mentally Ill Unit	33,793
Department of Mental Hygiene Expenditures	1,507,360
	$1,866,635

five-to-seven bed dormitory and observation area.

If prisoners become seriously disturbed in the course of serving their sentences, they are sometimes transferred out of the Department of Correctional Services into the legal custody of the State Office for Mental Health for treatment. Until 1977 these transferred prisoners were committed to Matteawan State Hospital; now they are put in the Central New York Psychiatric Center at Marcy, New York. Central New York has a capacity of 190 patients. The annual cost per patient is approximately $40,000, excluding fringe benefits and pension contributions. [33] (These costs have not been included in the cost of the New York State prison system.)

Central New York has a smaller capacity than Matteawan did before it closed (the average census of the latter was about 300 patients.)[34] When Matteawan closed, a number of seriously disturbed prisoners were sent back to the Department of Correctional Services and placed in its regular maximum-security prisons, where they mix with the general prisoner population. Green Haven and Fishkill Correctional Facilities absorbed the majority of these transfers, and Green Haven was handling about 50 percent of the psychiatric cases in the department in mid-1978.

The staff of this project visited Green Haven and learned that about 400 inmates there were being treated by the psychiatric unit, and about 100 were on medication. Some of the more severe cases were held in the eight-bed psychiatric unit.

Drug Addiction Therapy: According to the New York State Division of Substance Abuse, there were 11,400

persons in state prisons on July 1, 1977 who had
been identified as narcotics addicts before coming
to prison.[35] This represented about 60 percent of
the entire prisoner population at that time. Despite this, the *Department of Correctional Services operated no addiction treatment programs during fiscal 1978*. The
only opportunity for drug abuse therapy in prison
was provided by Reality House, Inc., a private organization. Counselors from this agency conducted
group therapy sessions in prison in addition to
their larger treatment program in New York City.
During 1977-78 sessions were conducted in nine state
prisons, but the small size of the program made it
impossible to service more than a handful of pris-
oner-addicts. During fiscal 1978 an estimated 562
prisoners were admitted to the group treatment program.[36] This constituted only 4% of those identified
as addicts prior to imprisonment.*

The Reality House prison program consists of a
weekly three-hour group therapy session which begins
at any point within a year of the prisoners' eligibility for parole. (This period will soon be limited to sixty days prior to parole eligibility.)
Addicts are encouraged to confront themselves and
the reasons for their addiction to drugs. Although
prisoners are no longer physically dependant upon
drugs while confined, they often return to the social milieu from which they originally came. Reality House attempts to help the prisoner avoid becoming re-addicted upon release.

During fiscal 1978 Reality House spent an estimated $75,000 on their prison therapy program.
Funding came from the State Division of Substance
Abuse Services (formerly the Office of Drug Abuse
Services in fiscal 1978), and the National Institute for Drug Abuse.[37] This expenditure represented
only .03 percent of the total cost of prisons in New
York State in fiscal 1978, or an average of $133 for
each of the 562 addict-prisoners in treatment.

Education: The high school diploma has become
the basic requirement for an extraordinarily wide

---

*Since fiscal 1978 drug treatment programs have ex-
panded. A pilot program at Arthur Kill, operated by
Therapeutic Communities, Inc., was established with
a capacity to service approximately 250 drug abusers. Counseling groups were also set up at five
other facilities. Reality House continues to serve
the majority of the few addicts in treatment.

variety of jobs in American society. Approximately
80 percent of New York state prisoners lack this
certification, however. Indeed, 22 percent stopped
their formal education in elementary school. [38] Many
are functionally illiterate and are incapable of
filling out job applications. This low education
level is not a reflection of intelligence, for the
I.Q. range of prisoners is similar to that of the
general American population.[39]

To provide educational opportunities for convicted prisoners, $6.6 million, or about $351 per
inmate, was spent by the Department of Correctional
Services during fiscal 1978 for academic and general
education. These expenditures are detailed in Table
2.13. (Costs incurred by other government agencies
such as state colleges are not included in these
figures.)

TABLE 2.13
Cost of Academic Education

Education Administration	$ 651,285
Academic and General Education	5,371,918
Music Education	95,114
Inmate Library	535,102
	$6,653,419

The majority of the students in the prison
schools are in classes studying for the High School
Equivalency Exam which requires only eighth-grade
competence in reading and mathematics. Upon successful completion of this exam, they receive a New
York State Regents General Education Diploma. Some
lower level students are in federally funded remedial instruction courses. VISTA volunteers also
teach basic literacy to about 1,000 prisoners.
Prisoners are enrolled in college courses taught inside the prison walls. As part of the temporary release program (to be described below), selected inmates are also allowed to leave the prisons during
the day to attend local colleges, but this program
has been cut back recently to the point of virtual
elimination.

Vocational Education: Three and a half decades ago, New York City Correction Commissioner Austin MacCormick wrote: "When we go into the occupational history of any prison population we find a tragic record of vocational incompetence."[40] New York State prisoners still fit this description. As noted in the beginning of this chapter, approximately 86 percent of the prisoner population was semiskilled or unskilled, and only 13 percent were permanently employed at time of arrest.

To remedy this "vocational incompetence," $5,295,095 was spent by the state prison system in fiscal 1978 for vocational education programs, exclusive of fringe and pension costs. This represented 2 percent of the total prison expenditures that year, and it averaged about $279 per inmate per year, excluding the wages paid to prisoners for attendance. This money was spent on 175 vocational shops in seventeen different prisons. These include masonry, baking, woodworking, upholstery, agriculture, brickmaking, drafting, TV and radio repair, sewing machine repair, printing, and metal fabrication, among others.[41]

One characteristic of the vocational training programs is that they are training inmates in several trades which offer little work in the free society. About a quarter of the shops teach construction trades. But construction has been a depressed industry in New York State for several years.[42] Throughout the United States there has been a pronounced shift in the job market away from manufacturing and agriculture toward the service sector. About three-quarters of New York State workers are employed in service industries.[43] Although the state prison system has established vocational training programs for some of these trades (e.g., television and auto repair, building maintenance), many of the nation's fastest growing service industries (e.g., health care services, information processing) are not represented in these programs. Indeed, many of the service trades currently being taught are those in *declining* industries. These include tailoring, barbering, cabinetmaking, shoe repair, baking, and sewing machine repair.[44] In short, New York prisons *are not adequately matching training programs with opportunities in the outside world.*

New York prison administrators recognize that vocational training needs upgrading, and federal grants have been obtained to improve the programs. Over $5 million in LEAA funds have been spent during the last three years to purchase new training equipment, to pay for the development of instructional modules, and to hire educational counselors. (About $1.3 million of these funds was spent during fiscal year 1978.)[45] But the more serious problem of matching vocational training to employment opportunities in the state needs attention. Investment in vocational training programs should reflect the prospective employment opportunities for ex-prisoners, forecasts of which require surveys of both job markets and labor pools. Current vocational training in New York State prisons does not take the realities of the labor market into account.

Temporary Release: In the late 1960s New York began a program which provided prisoners the opportunity for a graduated re-entry into their communities. The legislature passed a bill in 1968 allowing day release for work from jails in New York City and other local jurisdictions, and in 1969 a similar statute was enacted which applied to state prisoners. This law was amended in 1972 to allow other kinds of temporary release -- for education, volunteer service, leaves of absence, and overnight furloughs. To be eligible for temporary release, prisoners had to be within eighteen months of parole eligibility and had to be passed by a screening board. The 1972 laws also authorized the transfer of prisoners eligible for temporary release to "residential treatment facilities."[46] The Department of Correctional Services then acquired a number of urban properties and converted them into temporary-release facilities.

The temporary release program expanded quickly. In 1970 approximately thirty prisoners were granted work release from Auburn prison, and participation peaked in 1976. During that year approximately 8,000 prisoners in general confinement institutions were granted 16,800 furloughs. Another 8,554 prisoners were involved in educational or work release programs, many of them quartered in the urban temporary-release facilities.[47]

The legislature's commitment to temporary release has always been tentative, and the authorizing legislation was always written to require renewal after relatively short periods of time. A number of heavily publicized crimes by temporary-release prisoners coincided with the legislature's review of the statutes, and in 1977 the lawmakers severely restricted the program. The modified law shortens the eligibility period and requires the commissioner to personally approve the temporary release applicants

with serious crimes on their records. In consequence the program has withered. The preliminary
figures show that probably no more than 1,400 persons were involved in temporary-release programs
during 1978.[48]

In fiscal 1978 only $1,438,596 was spent on the
temporary-release program. This accounted for only
0.6 percent of the total expenditure for prisons.
Very few inmates are now released on work or educational release and several of the community-based
prisons have been closed. During fiscal 1978 only
3 percent of the prison population was housed in
these community prisons.[49]

Despite the crimes committed by a few prisoners on temporary release, the programs were generally successful from the point of view of public
safety. Of the 1,979 furloughs or leaves of absence granted in the first half of 1978, sixteen
were either arrested or absconded. Of those 926
prisoners granted work or educational release, industrial training or community service leave, elev-
en absconded or were arrested.[50]

One of the drawbacks of an extensive work-
release program is that many offenders have diffi-
culty finding work which continues to be attractive
after they are released from prison custody. One
solution might be the creation of a "supported work"
program for work-released prisoners. In Western
Europe, sheltered workshops (insulated from the full
rigors of the regular job market) exist for those
unable for various reasons to find and hold regular
employment. Here in the United States experimental
programs are showing that many hard-to-employ persons, including ex-offenders, can work effectively
under supportive conditions.[51] To make them attractive to employers who might not otherwise hire them,
supported workers are partially subsidized by public
monies. Those with poor work records and little experience are also supervised more closely as they
work in small teams. In many cases, the demonstration projects have had to create new jobs -- often
of a public works nature -- in order to avoid direct
competition with organized labor.

Although public subsidy of prisoner wages is
undoubtedly controversial, it is possible to design
a work-release program which would cost less than
the current $15,050 spent annually to house a single
prisoner, even with a wage subsidy. As we have
seen, the community-based facilities were even more
expensive to operate in fiscal 1978, but different
staffing patterns could lower the per prisoner cost

enough to produce the required savings. There is also evidence that supported work pays a dividend in crime reduction. One of the experimental projects compared two groups -- those who were randomly selected for the supported work program and those who were randomly rejected. The former worked more, earned more money, and were less frequently involved in criminal activity during the period they worked in the program.[52]

Religious Counseling and Services: During fiscal 1978 the Department of Correctional Services spent $1,344,850, or $71 per inmate, to provide prisoners the opportunity for spiritual development. The major portion of this ($848,213) was spent to support pastoral counseling, while the remainder went toward ministerial services.

Catholic and Protestant chaplains are generally available in each of the prisons, and the Bilalian (Black Muslim) and Sunni Muslim groups are usually led by fellow prisoners designated Imans, or spiritual leaders. (Prior to 1961, Muslims were considered to be subversive by prison administrators and Muslims practiced their religion covertly, under the threat of punishment. Freedom of religion was finally established as a result of court decisions in suits brought by Muslims.)[53]

Miscellaneous Other Program Costs: Two other small costs were not allocated to any of the other broad categories. These include $1,853 for occupational therapy and $88,685 for vocational rehabilitation. These total $90,538, or .04 percent of the total cost of imprisonment in fiscal 1978.

Prison Industries

New York State operates a number of factories within ten prisons: Attica, Clinton, Green Haven, Wallkill, Coxsackie, Eastern, Great Meadow, Bedford Hills, Auburn, Elmira, plus a distribution center in Menands. These industries do not provide work for many prisoners. There are only 1,500 industrial jobs throughout the state, enough to employ about 8 percent of the total prisoner population. Over seventy-five different products are made, including soap, brooms, roadside snow fences, garments, eyeglasses, desks, and picnic tables. The largest industrial shop is at Auburn, where inmates manufacture license plates, roadsigns, furniture, and repair auto bodies. Table 2.14 shows how industry

TABLE 2.14
Cost of New York Prison Industries, FY 1978
(excluding fringe and pension costs)

Administration and Support Services	$1,893,860
Supplies (general) (includes raw materials, machinery and equipment, including office equipment)	3,150,728
Shop Operation	8,297,189
Other	251,416
	13,593,193
Minus revenues generated from sale of products	-9,595,059
	$3,998,134

monies were spent in fiscal 1978.

The stated goals of the industries program are to (1) produce goods for the state at a reasonable cost, and (2) provide inmates with vocational training in marketable skills. [54] Unfortunately, neither is being accomplished. During fiscal 1978 the correctional industries lost money. Approximately $13.6 million was spent on the industries,* and only $9.6 million in revenues were produced from sales of goods to other public agencies.[55] This loss of

---

*Determining the cost of correctional industries during a single year is difficult because of the way raw materials and other supplies are stockpiled. Expenditures for industries might be artificially low in one year because a large portion of the expended supplies were bought in previous years. A precise computation of industry costs requires averaging expenditures and revenues over several consecutive years.

$4 million cannot be attributed to inflated wages,
for prisoners are paid between 8.75¢ and 28.75¢ per
hour. [56] Furthermore, prisoners for the most part
are not acquiring experience which can be carried
over to work in the free community.

Both of these failings can be traced to the
fact that prison labor programs were not originally
designed to assist prisoners upon release or to
train them in useful skills, but rather as activities to keep them busy while in confinement. Prisoners were also seen as sources of cheap labor for
the state. Although prison administrators now refer
to the "rehabilitative goals" of the industries,
these two original purposes continue to shape the
character of the system. They also tend to undercut
whatever potential for prisoner assistance and
training the system might have, as well as encourage
inefficient management.

In a report released in 1977 the New York Comptroller's Office criticized the industries program
for not having more management control over productivity. [57] The report also noted that the Auburn industries were heavily overstaffed, with idle men in-
terfering with the work of others. But the need for
creating work in prison to reduce the number of idle
hands makes this a difficult problem to rectify. In
addition to devising ways of increasing prisoner interest and productivity, the prison system must expand the opportunities for work. Without this, increasing labor productivity merely expands the pool
of idle inmates and increases the potential for
riot.

Mismanagement: Until very recently, industries
management has not been visible to outsiders. Since
the beginnings of the industries program in 1893 until 1974, the program was supported by a revolving
fund. [58] Only for the past four years has the legislature made regular appropriations for this item.
The State Comptroller's Office has made several audits and has suggested a number of changes in
management. [59]

According to the audits, many management deficiencies could be corrected. These included: [60]

- Raw materials purchases were based on unre-
  liable forecasts and the inventory records
  were inaccurate.

- Bills of materials, listing the components
  in each finished product, did not exist for

most products. Production standards and
shop quotas did not exist.

- The Fiscal Unit did not maintain adequate
or up-to-date records.

- Product selling prices were not based on
accurate or up-to-date financial data.
In fact, several products were being sold
below manufacturing costs. The Marketing
Unit established product selling prices
based on "guesstimates" or a 20-year-old
cost formula.

- The division's promotional activities
were excessive. The audit noted an instance where $600 of merchandise was
given as samples to an agency in consid-
cration of a $2,400 order. Discounted
items were given away rather than being
sold at a discount...For example, office
furniture valued at $560 was in effect
given to a state agency for use in a
deputy commissioner's office.

To increase management control over the industries, the department has begun to install a new
computerized financial management system. Prices of
goods have also been updated.

The State-Use System: At the heart of the prison
labor problem -- both the vocational training program and the industries -- are the severe legal restrictions on prisoners' work. Prisoners are not
allowed to compete with laborers in the outside society. A New York Constitutional Convention in 1894
wrote an amendment to the state constitution forbid-
ding prison labor to be "farmed out, given or
sold..." [61] Since then, prison goods can only be
sold to the state or its political subdivisions, including local government agencies, although license
plates are sold to other states.

Remedying the prison labor problem could begin
with various legislative changes. These include:

- enabling legislation to encourage the involvement of private industry in prisons;
- modifying the state-use laws to allow the
sale of prison goods to other states and
to the federal government;
- legislation permitting the sale of inmate

goods on the free market; to gain organized labor's approval of this, it would
probably be necessary to pay inmates
competitive wages;
- legislation clarifying the inmate's status
regarding workman's compensation;
- legislation modifying the procurement
operations of prisons to expedite pur-
chasing and discourage hoarding.

Even in the absence of legislative changes,
however, a more relevant and efficient industrial
program could be established in prisons by administrative reforms. State and local governments continue to grow rapidly, and these are expanding
markets for a wide variety of goods. Prison industry administrators could be more aggressive in determining which new products could be produced in
prison and distributed to this market.

Prison administrators could also forge a useful
link between the vocational training shops and work
in industries. At present there is little training
in the industries, and no formally programmed se-
quence to move a prisoner from vocational training
shops to the industries. A more effective job
skills program would provide vocational training and
then the opportunity to put these newly acquired
skills to work in an industrial setting.

Another industrial reform has been developed by
ECON, Inc., a private organization.[62] Their "free
venture model" has been demonstrated in Connecticut
with federal government support and is now being du-
plicated on an experimental basis in Colorado, Illi-
nois, Iowa, Minnesota, and Washington. In this model many of the essential features of industry in the
free community are reproduced in prisons. These include:

- industries operate on a profit or break-
even basis
- prisoners are trained in trades which are
transferable to outside employment
- a full day's work
- prisoners' wages based on work output
- wages approaching those of private industry
- productivity standards comparable to those
of private industry
- hire and fire procedures, within the limits
of due process

The capacity of these reforms to increase the

number of jobs in prisons and to teach prisoners
marketable trades should be closely examined by New
York prison administrators.

Miscellaneous Costs

A number of other miscellaneous costs cannot be sen-
sibly distributed among the five broad classes of
activities (security, administration and overhead,
necessities, programs, and industry). These include
the costs of special housing, which serve both medical and security (i.e., disciplinary) functions,
elderly and handicapped, and the reimbursements to
Nassau County for housing state prisoners. All
costs not assigned to the five broad activity classes are shown in Table 2.15.

TABLE 2.15
Miscellaneous Expenses

Board of Prisoners	$ 22,984
Housing (Nassau County only)	73,000
Judgments	21,021
Small Claims	12,847
Special Housing	135,216
Elderly and Handicapped	56,527
Parole Information	1,680
Undistributed	44,415
Advances	32,276
Varied Other Expenses	155,103
	$555,069

The Cost of Expanding the State Prison System

Since 1973 the state prison population in New York
has been expanding rapidly. Penalties for a number
of offenses were made more stringent by laws established in 1973 and again in 1978, and the prison
system will have to expand quickly to accommodate
the expected increase in prisoners.[63] This section
reviews the prisoner population trends, the expansion of the state prison system in the 1970s, and
the planned costs of further expansion.

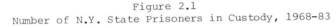

Figure 2.1
Number of N.Y. State Prisoners in Custody, 1968-83

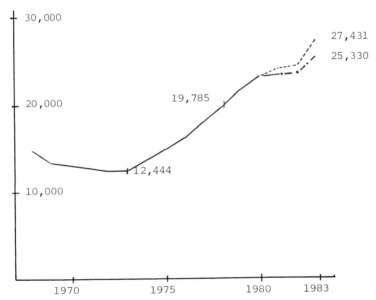

1968-78: Population on January 1
1979-83: Projected population, Dept. of Correctional Services
-------- High projection
—.—.—. Low projection

Source: Department of Correctional Services: "Admissions
and Releases from Facilities of the Department of Correctional
Services for the Calendar Years 1968-1977," and "Violent Felony Offender Law: Impact on DOCS Population from New Sentence
Structure," (July 27, 1978).

For several years prior to 1973 the state had successfully reduced the number of inmates in its prison system. Figure 2.1 shows that the prisoner population reached a low point in 1973, when the January 1 census for that year stood at 12,444.[64] But 1973 saw the passage of the most severe drug laws in the nation, prescribing mandatory imprisonment for long terms. Persons convicted of a second felony within ten years also became subject to mandatory prison terms. Between January 1, 1973 and October 16, 1978 the state prisoner population increased 60 percent, from 12,444 to 20,500. [65]

To house these prisoners the State Department of Correctional Services opened fourteen new prisons between 1973 and 1978. Many of these were buildings acquired from the State Office of Drug Abuse Services, which had used these buildings to house drug addicts who had been committed (by civil rather than criminal procedures) to compulsory drug treatment. With the 1973 drug legislation, the experiment with civil commitment ended and drug offenders were sent to prison. The Office of Drug Abuse Services buildings were than transferred to the Department of Correctional Services and converted into prisons.

A new maximum-security prison (Downstate Correctional Facility) with a capacity of 1,080 prisoners was also built with a total appropriation for construction of $48.4 million, or about $45,000 per cell.[66] It is scheduled for completion and opening in 1979.

The growth of the state prisoner population shows no sign of abating. Indeed, the legislature passed the Omnibus Crime Control Bill in 1978 and this will insure that the bumper crop in corrections will grow at an even faster rate in the future. The penalties were escalated for so-called "violent felonies," for violent felony repeaters, and for violent juveniles. Again, mandatory prison terms were instituted for a wide range of offenses, along with higher maximum sentences. Plea bargaining is restricted after indictment to attempt to limit the possibility of defendants' escaping prison by negotiating.

How the prosecutors and the courts will adapt to these new laws is unclear, but it is very likely that many more people will be going to prison for longer periods of time. [67] After a delay of two or three years, the lengthier sentences imposed under the new law will most likely produce a skyrocketing of prisoner populations. The Department of Correc-

tional Services estimates that over 27,000 inmates
will be crowding the state prisons in 1983 if there
is maximum compliance with the letter and spirit of
the new law. [68] If, however, half of those booked
for violent felonies manage to escape prison by pre-
indictment bargaining, there will still be over
25,000 persons in prison in 1983. After 1983 the
prisoner population will increase at an even *faster*
rate if the expected practices continue in the same
direction. (Note the steep slope of the projected
curves in Figure 2.1.)

To house this rapidly growing population of
state prisoners, the Department of Correctional
Services is planning two different expansion strategies. The first involves the leasing of Rikers Island, a penal complex currently operated by the New
York City Department of Correction. The second
calls for construction of new prisons. Both of
these are extraordinarily expensive propositions.

The Rikers Island transfer envisions a phased
takeover whereby 1,320 beds would be turned over to
the state in 1980. [69] The city would then begin construction and rehabilitation of replacement cells
for its own prisoner population. (See Chapter 6 for
further discussion.) The state would occupy the remaining 3,100 cells in several stages after the city
acquires replacement cells.

The state government will pay $200 million for
the use of Rikers, plus an estimated $100 million
for renovating the buildings. Further, the state
has agreed to make available to New York City a
number of smaller facilities if it needs additional
cell space during the transition. The cost of leasing and upgrading the Rikers Island facilities
amounts to approximately $65,000 per cell, not
counting the possible high costs of financing (to be
discussed below).

Even if the transfer of Rikers Island to the
state is accomplished, the state prison system will
still not be able to meet its longer term demands
for space if the imprisonment trends continue as
projected. To expand capacity still further, the
Department of Correctional Services and consulting
architects have developed a Construction Action
Plan. [70] This plan offers three alternative programs
and recommends as the optimal strategy a three-year
expansion of nine existing prisons, adding 3,080
maximum-security cells to the state system. In January 1978 the projected cost for this expansion was
estimated at $94.1 million, or $30,600 per cell.
The actual cost of any new prison construction will

be *much* higher, however, even in the very near future. There are several reasons for this:

- The general rule of thumb is that capital
  costs are usually underestimated so that
  the project will be approved. The nearly
  inevitable "overruns" are considered a
  normal feature of construction.

- Inflation will drive the cost higher than
  initially projected. The architects' estimates were based on 1977 construction costs.
  Since then, the average cost of construction has been increasing at the annual rate
  of about 12 percent. If prison construction
  were to begin in 1981, it would cost approximately *$48,150* to build what would have
  cost $30,600 in 1977.

- The cost of furnishing the prisons was excluded from the construction costs. This
  could easily equal 10 percent of construction costs.

- Architects' fees were also excluded from
  these initial estimates. These will vary
  depending upon the size of the project
  and the amount of planning to be done, but
  it is reasonable to anticipate their being
  about 10 percent of the cost of construction.

- Finally, the extremely high cost of financing can quadruple the ultimate cost to the
  taxpayers of building prisons. If the state
  government decides to borrow money in order
  to finance construction or acquisition of
  prisons, a bond issue will be offered to
  raise the needed revenues. Buyers in effect
  lend money to the state at interest. The
  state pays them back over a long period of
  time, using funds generated from taxes. The
  total amount the state ultimately spends over
  the long run depends on the length of the
  repayment period and the interest rate. Debt
  for prison construction is likely to be
  stretched out for a very long time, perhaps
  thirty or forty years. (The longer the
  period, the lower the annual repayments will
  be.) The interest rate depends upon the market conditions at the time of the bond of-
  fering. It is likely that the state will

have to borrow at a rate of at least
8 or 9 percent.

Tables 2.16 and 2.17 summarize these additional
expenses which could ultimately quadruple the cost
of building prisons above and beyond the initial
construction costs. For the sake of illustration,
the tables assume that the actual construction cost
is $48,150 per cell, or the equivalent in 1981 dol-
lars of the Construction Action Plan's optimal projection. It also omits cost overruns because these
are difficult to estimate.

TABLE 2.16
Upstate Prison Expansion: Component Costs
of Building in Early 1980s

Component	Estimated Cost per Cell
Construction	$48,150
Architects' fees, planning, site development	4,815
Furnishing	4,815
	$57,780

TABLE 2.17
Cost of Financing Upstate Prison Expansion
Where Construction Costs Equal $57,780 Per Cell

Repayment Period (in Years)	Interest Rate	Average Annual Installment	Total Financing Cost per Cell
30	8%	$5,088	$152,636
30	9	5,579	167,363
40	8	4,819	192,754
40	9	5,346	213,832

The preferred arrangement for the state would be the longer repayment period at the lower rate. This would run the cost up to *four times* the initial construction costs. A 9 percent rate would require the taxpayer to spend *440 percent more* than the initial construction expense.

The precise scenario to be followed remains uncertain. It is clear, however, that state prison capacity will be expanded rapidly by one means or another in the very near future unless immediate reforms are made in sentencing and parole policies. During 1978 the governor recommended acquiring Rikers Island, renovating Ossining, and appropriating $55 million to build two new 512-bed maximum-security prisons adjacent to the existing Woodbourne and Wallkill facilities, and the immediate opening of a new 1,000-bed facility at Fishkill. The state legislature approved the construction of only one new facility, but in all other respects accepted the governor's recommendations without extensive analysis of need or fiscal implications.

Prison expansion is a very costly venture. Not only are the initial costs high, but the cost of financing and operating the prisons places a continuing and heavy mortgage on the future. Prisons have a very long life and, once built, they will be difficult to close. Reducing the reach of the prison system once it has expanded is an increasingly unlikely prospect. For example, the first New York State prison (Auburn) was built in 1817 and is still in use.

Despite the Department of Correctional Services

projections, the anticipated increases in the prisoner population are not inevitable. Changes in sentencing and parole policies could either stablize or
reduce the numbers of persons in prison, thereby
lowering the cost to the taxpayer without measurably
affecting public safety.

SUMMARY

New York State's largest corrections expense is its
prison system. During fiscal 1978 taxpayers spent
$285.5 million, or $15,050 per person to keep an
average of 18,968 convicted felons behind bars for a
single year. This average cost masks a wide range
of costs from one prison to another: from $9,539 in
the least expensive prison to $39,018 in the most
expensive.
    Much of the difference in cost is explained by
how heavily the prison is staffed. This is because
about 80 percent of the total spending for state
prisons was for salaries and fringe benefits. On
the average, there were two staff persons for every
three prisoners during fiscal 1978. In the less expensive prisons the ratio of staff to prisoners was
much lower, while the reverse was true in the more
expensive.
    Despite these high costs, life in state prison
is far from luxurious. Only $1.83 was spent each
day, or $666 annually, on food for each prisoner.
Health care cost $532 per prisoner per year, mostly
for medical staff salaries. In contrast, an annual
average of $7,525 per prisoner was spent on security
costs (mostly guards' salaries and benefits). Another $3,311 per prisoner was spent on administra-
tion and processing convicts through the system. In
total: about 87 percent or $13,090 of the total an-
nual cost per prisoner was spent simply to keep
inmates alive, fed, and under guard.
    Even though most prisoners are uneducated, un-
skilled, and were unemployed before coming to prison, proportionately little money ($1,505 per prison-
er or 10 percent of the total) is spent on programs
to alleviate these handicaps. For example, 11,400
prisoners were reported to be addicted to narcotics
at the time of their arrest, but only 562 were receiving treatment for their drug abuse during fiscal

1978 . Moreover, these few that were getting treatment were in a program operated and funded not by the prisons but by an outside private organization.

Many of the prison programs that are ostensibly aimed at providing opportunities for self-betterment are poorly designed or badly managed. Several vocational training shops are teaching prisoners skills in trades which are shrinking and promise little chance of work after release. Vocational training is not effectively linked to work programs in the prison. The industries which do exist behind the walls require little training and give prisoners few skills which can be used in the outside world. These industries are not only poor training centers; they are also *costing* money rather than making it. During fiscal 1978 industries spent $13.6 million and earned only $9.6 million from the sale of products. In short: the pattern of spending in state prisons shows that the first priority is securely isolating criminal offenders rather than assisting their self-improvement.

Even though there is little evidence that imprisonment significantly reduces crime, lawmakers and judges are increasing their reliance on this most expensive sanction. The New York state prisoner population had been shrinking until 1972, when there were approximately 12,500 in custody at any one time. Since then a series of laws has been passed which prescribes mandatory terms of imprisonment and longer sentences. The prisoner population increased to 20,500 in late 1978, making the New York prisoner population the second largest in the country. To accommodate this increase, the state prison system expanded at a rate more rapid than at any time since its inception 150 years ago. As noted above, planners anticipate that the impact of a new 1978 law mandating stiffer penalties will send even more people to prison, perhaps as many as 25,000 to 27,000 by 1983. Plans are underway to construct and purchase new prisons at a minimum construction cost of $58,000 per bed. Financing this construction through bond issues could quadruple this cost.

3
Parole

During fiscal 1978 the New York State Division of
Parole spent $21 million, making it the least expen-
sive component of the state criminal corrections
agencies. However, the real significance of parole
for corrections costs is much greater than this
small budget indiciates because Parole Board decisions affect the size of the prisoner population.
Whereas judges have the power to send convicted persons to prison, the board has the power to determine
when they will be released from incarceration.*
    The impact of this parole release decision on
prison finances is considerable. Had the Parole
Board required all those paroled during 1976 to
serve only another three months before being released, the prisons would have had to absorb an additional 1,100 convict-years of sentenced prisoners
-- enough to fill a medium-sized prison.[1] This
would have cost the prison system an additional
$16.6 million in operating expenses alone, not
counting the high cost of constructing or acquiring
these cells. [2]
    The power of the Parole Board to release pris-
oners has come under attack in recent years, and a
movement is underway to abolish the board's discretionary release powers altogether. Such a reform
could have an enormous impact on the size and cost
of the prison system. Under current practice court-

---

*The Parole Board does not see the explicit regula-
tion of prisoner population as one of its mandates;
indeed, it insists that the decisions about individual cases *not* be affected by prison management concerns. These thousands of individual decisions have
an important impact on the size of the prisoner
population, however.

57

imposed maximum sentences are almost never fully served in prison. Prisoners are either paroled after serving a portion (generally a third to a half) of the imposed maximum, or are conditionally released after serving their maximum sentences minus whatever "good-time" credit they have accumulated.* (The remainder of their sentences is served in the community under parole supervision.) An elimination of Parole Board release authority must be accompanied by a reduction in the *length of maximum sentences imposed* by the court. Failure to reduce sentences will significantly increase the *actual length of time served* at enormous cost to the taxpayer. Although the existing data cannot tell us exactly how much more time would be served, a rough estimate is that prisoners released by the Parole Board in 1976 would have had to serve an average of ten to twelve months more in prison if parole release were not possible.[3] The number of prisoners in custody would have been approximately 25 percent higher at the end of the year. This would have required an estimated additional cost to the state prison system of $60.2 to $75.3 million that year, not counting the cost of constructing or acquiring the needed cell space.[4]

This chapter

- shows how much the Division of Parole spent during fiscal 1978 to accomplish each of its primary tasks;
- reviews the cost and nature of parole supervision;
- examines the tension between the Parole Board as a sentencing agency and its de facto role in regulating prisoner population and cost; and
- briefly reviews the move to abolish or sharply reduce discretionary parole authority.

---

*Prisoners are conditionally released after serving two-thirds of their court-imposed maximum sentences unless the prison officials reduce their good-time credits for disciplinary infractions.

The Organization and Cost of Parole

The Division of Parole is an agency of the state
government Executive Department which employed about
1,000 persons during fiscal 1978. [5] The work of the
division is focused on three principal activities:
sentencing,* parole supervision, and administration.
Table 3.1 shows the estimated expenditure in fiscal
1978 for each of these three tasks.[6]

TABLE 3.1
Cost of Different Parole Activities in New York State, FY 1978

Administration		$ 1,191,200 (6%)
Sentencing		
Parole Board	777,042	
LEAA grant	231,011	
Field parole investigation	1,462,345	
Institutional parole	3,305,702	
Department of Mental Health	210,000	
		5,986,100 (28%)
Supervision in the community		14,026,100 (66%)
		$21,203,400 (100%)

Sources: Computed from information supplied by the Division
of Parole, letters of June 13 and June 30, 1978, and telephone
conversation of November 24, 1978. See note 6 for description
of estimating procedures. Department of Mental Health Data
from NYS Department of Mental Health, Bureau of Forensic Psychiatry, personal communication, October 6, 1978.

---

*Under the current penal statutes, only the courts
have the *formal* authority to impose sentence, and the
parole boards have the power to determine the length
of imprisonment (within certain boundaries imposed
by the courts). Throughout this report the power to
fix the length of prison confinement is considered a
sentencing function. Therefore, "sentencing" refers
to *both* the courts' de jure authority to commit convicted persons to prison/jail and the Parole Board's
authority to determine the date of release. [7]

The Cost of Parole Board Sentencing

The sentencing duties of the Parole Board absorbed
about 28 percent of the division's fiscal 1978 operating expenditures, or nearly $6 million. The board
is the largest in the nation, and its twelve members
are appointed by the governor and approved by the
State Senate for terms of six years. It makes three
distinct types of sentencing decisions. It sets the
date of earliest parole eligibility for prisoners
who did not have minimum sentences established by
the courts. It determines the actual time to be
served in prison.* It also has the power to revoke
parole when the conditions of release are violated
in an important respect, sending the offender back
to prison.[8]
        During calendar year 1977 three-member panels
of the board held 3,553 hearings to fix parole eligibility dates, 10,580 hearings to consider parole
release, and 2,089 revocation hearings.[9] As a result, 4,851 state prisoners were released on original parole, and another 922 were released who had
been re-incarcerated for earlier violations of parole.** The board also released nearly 800 prisoners from the county jails and penitentiaries.[11]
        Assisting the board in its sentencing duties
are 105 institutional parole officers working in

---

*The board determines release in two ways. It can
either parole the prisoner, in which case it establishes the precise time of release, or it can with-
hold parole. In the latter case, the board is requiring the prisoner to serve the maximum sentence
or to be conditionally released by the Department of
Correctional Services. Conditional release dates
depend upon the prison keepers' award or stripping
of "good-time" credits, and the maximum sentence is
determined by the judge. By refusing to parole a
prisoner, the board is not directly fixing the precise date of release but is requiring the prisoner
to serve the maximum time possible. In these instances it is fair to say that the board is fixing
the time to be served, although it is not the
agency taking the responsibility for this later
release.
**Another 1,528 state prisoners who were refused
parole by the board were conditionally released to
parole supervision by the Department of Correctional
Services.[10]

twenty-four state prisons.[12] Shortly before their
parole hearings, prisoners are interviewed by these
institutional parole officers who compile a case
file describing the prisoner's criminal history, social background, adjustment to prison life, and
plans for the future. This record is read by the
Parole Board members during the hearings. Approximately 11,600 of these "investigations" were completed in 1977.[13]

Also included in the cost of the division's
sentencing duties are $231,000 in federal Law En-
forcement Assistance Administration (LEAA) monies
spent during fiscal 1978 for developing parole sentencing decision guidelines. The Bureau of Forensic
Psychiatry in the State Department of Mental Health
spent $210,000 to provide psychiatric reports on
certain prisoners about to be considered for release.* An estimated $1.46 million was spent by the
field parole officers investigating and approving
prospective homes and jobs for prisoners nearing
their parole release hearing. This information is
communicated to the institutional parole officers,
who in turn pass it on to the Parole Board.

The Cost and Character of Parole Supervision

Two-thirds, or $14 million, of the Division of Pa-
role operating expenditures in fiscal 1978 went for
supervising released prisoners in the community.

Approximately 60 percent of the costs of supervision was incurred by the New York City offices.[14]
This corresponds to the distribution of parolees
throughout the state, for approximately 60 percent
of the parole caseload is supervised in New York
City.[15] After release from prison to the custody of
the Division of Parole, the convict is supervised by
one of 348 field officers headquartered in eleven
cities across the state: New York City, Albany,
Binghamton, Buffalo, Canton, Elmira, Hempstead,
Poughkeepsie, Rochester, Syracuse, and Utica.[16]
About half the convicts released from state prison
in 1976 by the Parole Board had to serve between
twelve and thirty months on parole before completing
their sentences.[17] Most of the others had to serve
more time, with about 10 percent on lifetime parole.[18] There were almost 19,000 persons under ac-

---

*Law and executive orders mandate psychiatric re-
ports for persons convicted of sex offenses and
and homicide.

tive parole supervision for at least part of 1977,
with an average of 12,877 at any one time. [19]

As noted above, the average annual cost of
supervising one parolee in the community was *$1,090
during fiscal 1978*. (It is important to note that this
is an *average* annual cost, and that the actual costs
vary widely from one parolee to another.)   To con-
serve resources, the parole officers vary the supervision of parolees on the basis of perceived risk.
The supervision of cases thought to be riskier might
be as high as $5,000 apiece, whereas the cost of
supervising those deemed less risky might be as low
as a few hundred dollars.

During 1977 and 1978 there were three different
classes of supervision: intensive, active, and reduced. [20] These differ in the frequency of required
contact with the parolee and his or her family.
Intensive supervision involves weekly or semimonthly
contact, with the parole officer making at least one
monthly visit to the home, one to the parolee's
place of employment, and one parolee visit to the
local field office. This close supervision usually
lasts for only the first three months after release
from prison, the period in which violations occur
most frequently. [21] Parolees on *active* supervision
must make monthly visits to the parole office and
the parole officer must make one monthly visit to
the parolee's home and place of work. After a year
of successful active supervision, parolees may be
put on *reduced* status. This requires only quarterly
reporting. In 1979 the division added a fourth category for the future: *enhanced* supervision will en-
tail even closer surveillance than what was routine
in 1978, and it will probably cost even more.

The purpose of parole supervision is to protect
the community by controlling the parolee and to assist the successful reintegration of released prisoners into the community. The parole officers' task
is thus part law enforcement and part social work.
There is a good deal of tension between the require-
ments of these two roles, and in New York State the
balance tends to be struck in favor of law enforcement.

Before being released from prison, the convict
must sign an agreement to conform to a variety of
conditions. These include not traveling outside a
narrowly restricted geographical area without the
prior permission of the parole officer, avoiding the
excessive use of alcoholic beverages, avoiding the
company of persons having criminal records, and ob-
taining the parole officer's permission to marry,

divorce, change addresses, and change jobs. More generally, the parolee is required to "fully comply with the instruction of [the] parole officer."[22] Failure to comply with any of these conditions can result in a declaration of delinquency and the re-incarceration of the parolee.

The emphasis on law enforcement over more traditional social work services is reinforced by several formal rights and responsibilities of the parole officer. Officers are allowed to carry guns, and they are required to maintain proficiency in their use. They are also given broad authority to search both the physical person and residence of the parolee without a warrant. Parole officers also have the power to take the parolee into custody.

Parole supervision is essentially coercive, involving as it does an explicit threat of being sent back to prison for failing to comply with the conditions of parole. Relatively few positive kinds of services are provided. Indeed, there is a built-in conflict between traditional social work counseling and the more police-like aspects of parole. Effective counseling is aided by a bond of trust between the client and the social worker. Trust is difficult to establish when the parole officer has such fear-inspiring power over the parolee's future.

The resources available to parole officers for adequate social services are also very limited. Released inmates are given only $40 by the prison authorities as they leave prison and go back into the world. The Division of Parole cannot financially assist the parolee, except for making an emergency loan of $9 and referring him to the welfare department. The job-finding abilities of the division are also poorly developed. During 1976 parole officers made only 247 verified job placements of released prisoners.[23] Similarly, the division has a very limited ability to supply parolees with housing. Fifty-six beds in YMCAs exist for those who cannot find other residences.

It is possible that a stronger commitment by the Division of Parole to job placement could yield more employment for released prisoners, but the larger problem of declining opportunities for unskilled and semiskilled labor is beyond the division's ability to solve. What is needed is a more effective program of vocational training while in prison and perhaps a program of "supported work" for those parolees unable to find suitable work in the regular job market. As noted in Chapter 2, supported work programs for ex-offenders have shown themselves to be successful in deterring criminal activity during the course of employment. Although supported work programs are more expensive than other jobs because they require subsidies and closer supervision, they might keep enough ex-offenders and parolees out of prison to make them cost-effective.[24]

Finally, the question of whether parole supervision "works" is a matter of controversy. Some studies have shown that parole supervision does not significantly alter the arrest rates of released prisoners, whereas other studies claim an effect.[25] Continued research is needed.

The Tension Between Sentencing Authority and the Regulation of Prison Costs

Although parole boards regulate the size and cost of prisons by their individual parole release decisions, the board in New York sees this regulatory action more as an incidental consequence of its primary task -- the assessment of individual parole cases. Indeed, the law insists that individual parole decisions should not be used as a disciplinary tool for punishing or rewarding prisoners; neither should it be responsive to prison overcrowding.* The statute requires that:

> Discretionary release on parole shall not
> be granted merely as a reward for good
> conduct or efficient performance of duties
> while confined but after considering if
> there is a reasonable probability that, if
> such inmate is released, he will live and
> remain at liberty without violating the law,
> and that his release is not incompatible
> with the welfare of society and will not so
> deprecate the seriousness of his crime as

---

*A 1976 survey of Parole Board attitudes by the Citizens' Inquiry on Parole found that all board members agreed with the statement that "parole board policies should be basically independent of the immediate administrative needs of the Department of Correctional Services."

to undermine respect for the law. [26]

Despite the demand that individual parole decisions be based on a well-reasoned assessment of the individual prisoner, there has long been tension between prison management concerns and the need to insulate parole release decisions from these "extraneous" pressures. Until the 1970s parole reform revolved around trying to find the most appropriate organizational relationship between parole and prison administration. [27]

Parole release began in New York in 1889, and power was vested in the hands of the prison administrators. It was undoubtedly a welcome addition to their efforts to control population and management problems. As Professor Caleb Foote phrased it, "Nirvana for a prison warden would be exclusive jurisdiction over discharges." [28] Nirvana ended in 1929 when Governor Roosevelt appointed a blue ribbon panel to investigate the abuses of this power. The panel recommended the establishment of a parole board in an independent agency, arguing that "the work of such a Board should not be subordinated to the routine of purely custodial problems. Recent experience has indicated that this danger is incurred when parole is made a mere incident of the Correctional Department." [29] This recommendation was followed and the Division of Parole was established in the Executive Department in 1930.

Four decades later, in 1971, parole and prison administration were wed once again to "provide greater coordination and continuity in institutional and field supervisory services for those convicted criminals who require imprisonment." [30] The marriage was not a happy one, however. The 1970s saw increasing numbers of convicts sent to prison by the courts, and the principal problem of prison administrators has been managing a severely overcrowded system. The Parole Board responded to the "law and order" temper of the public by becoming more conservative in its parole release decisions. [31] The inevitable consequence of this policy was to exacerbate overcrowding by keeping prisoners behind bars for longer periods of time. Moreover, the almost completely unbounded discretion of the Parole Board made prison planning an extremely frustrating task. Not being able to predict either future parole policy or individual parole release decisions, prison administrators could not know precisely how long prisoners would remain in their custody.

The conflicts between prison and parole man-

agers became acrimonious and more public, and the
chief prison administrator finally called for abol-
ishing the Parole Board's authority.* Once again
the partnership was broken by the legislature, and
in 1978 the Division of Parole was born again in the
Executive Department. Lawmakers noted that "the
present organizational structure is not conducive to
the optimum performance of the parole system...."[33]
By separating parole from prison management, the Division of Parole would achieve a "necessary measure
of independence from the Department of Correctional
Services...."[34] The outcome of this independence has
been to formalize once again the fragmentation of
responsibility for criminal justice costs in New
York.

The Movement to
Abolish Parole Release Authority

Many reformers are calling for an end to the arrangement whereby sentencing authority is split between the judiciary and parole boards.[35] In a report issued in early 1979 the blue ribbon Executive
Advisory Committee on Sentencing appointed by the
governor concluded that the Parole Board decision
"re-sentences offenders on substantially the same
criteria employed by the sentencing judge." It
termed this arrangement "duplicative," which implies
-- by extension -- that its activies are an unnecessary expense. They recommended that the Parole
Board be stripped of its discretionary release authority and that the judiciary fix the actual time
to be served in prison.[36]
    This represents a dramatic reversal of a hun-
dred-year trend. Over the past several decades the
constitutionality of parole release authority had

---

*Conflict was not only over release policies but al-
so over budgets. Three months after the 1971 merger
the Attica prison riots occurred. The Department of
Correctional Services spent most of its reserves on
in-prison programs, leaving postrelease parole a low
priority. Parole administrators felt that independence from the department would bring a higher level
of funding.[32]

been legitimated by a theory of corrections which had a compelling logic. This theory asserted that the prime purpose of imprisonment was the rehabilitation of criminal offenders. Since judges could only guess how quickly such a process might occur, they set only the outer limits of time to be served. (Sentences are thus "indeterminate.") The task of determining when prisoners were successfully "cured" belonged to parole authorities.

In the mid-1970s this division of sentencing authority and its legitimizing rationale came under heavy criticism. The Citizens' Inquiry on Parole and Criminal Justice, Inc., published its report on New York parole in 1975 and found that Parole Board discretionary release decisions were excessively arbitrary and founded on unwarranted assumptions.

> Parole in New York rests on faulty theory and has unrealistic goals. The humanitarian goal of treatment and rehabilitation of the offender has been used to justify unnecessarily lengthy incarceration and parole supervision. Since there is no agreement on the meaning of rehabilitation and no one now knows what rehabilitates or who is rehabilitated, decisions as to length of sentence and timing of release based on an assessment of an inmate's rehabilitation are irrational and cruel. [37]

The proposed alternative was the elimination of indeterminate sentencing practices in New York.

In 1976 the staff of the Codes Committee of the New York State Assembly issued a highly critical report and a call for legislative reform of parole without abandoning it completely.

> One of the most accurate and frequent criticisms of the New York State Board of Parole is the unguided manner in which it makes minimum period of imprisonment and release decisions. Are we to believe that the Board makes accurate, fair, and uniform decisions when it follows no specific written criteria, spends only a few moments with each inmate and his file, utilizes no predictive devices, sets unrealistic minimum periods of imprisonment and then refuses to release the inmate at his first release hearing because of his past record and the severity of his offense,

and allows the courts to set the tone for
minimal due process standards at their
hearings? We cannot believe it, and we
cannot urge strongly enough that the time
is long overdue for reform of the Board's
decision making process. [38]

In consequence the legislature passed a law in
1977 requiring the Parole Board to establish decision guidelines that explicitly account for the
seriousness of the crime and the offender's previous
criminal history. [39] (The U.S. Board of Parole instituted similar guidelines in 1972.) To develop
these guidelines the Division of Parole obtained a
grant from LEAA. [40] (See Table 3.1 for fiscal 1978
expenditures.) A gridded table was designed speci-
fying ranges of actual prison time to be served for
different levels of offense severity and different
types of criminal records. These suggested terms
are intended only as *guides* rather than prescrip-
tions. Parole release authority in New York remains
discretionary, although the setting of parole *eligibility* dates is now more structured than it was in
the past.

In 1978 the Special Committee on Criminal Sentencing convened by The Correctional Association of
New York called for a similar abolition of parole
release authority in New York and the establishment
of determinate sentencing procedures. [41] It recommended that the legislature create a Sentencing
Guideline Commission empowered to determine the alternative sanctions for each type of crime. Sanctions should not be based, as they are in the current indeterminate sentencing schemes, on the perceived rehabilitative needs of the offender. Rather, they should be proportionate to the seriousness
of the offense itself and the offender's prior criminal record.

The Division of Parole has attempted to meet
these criticisms by articulating new guidelines for
parole eligibility. Moving away from the traditional role of assessing the "treatment success" of
prisoners, these guidelines are based only on seriousness of offense and prior criminal record. "In
no way," said the chairman of the Parole Board, do
board members "attempt to predict future behavior." [42]

By abandoning the goal of rehabilitation, the
Parole Board has lost the rationale which histori-
cally justified the division of sentencing authority
between it and the courts. Many critics argue

that the Parole Board should therefore be stripped
of the discretionary power to release prisoners.
Judging from the experience of states which have
done so, however, there is good reason to hesitate
before embracing this solution, for, if adopted,
prisoners are likely to spend more time behind bars.
It swells prisoner populations and costs, while
yielding a relatively insignificant dividend in reduced crime rates.

Many advocates of determinate sentencing and
the abolition of discretionary parole release authority demand that this reform not be accompanied by
longer sentences. [43] This proviso is turning out to
be a hard one to meet. Under indeterminate sentencing systems, both the legislatures and the courts
have been able to mandate stiff sentences which are
more symbolic than real, for prisoners almost never
serve them in full. To begin reckoning sentences in
"real" time rather than these symbolic maximums is
a politically difficult task. It is hard to make
the shift without a seeming reduction in the length
of criminal sentences. In California, for example,
this shift to "real" time generated strong public
pressures to push the mandated sentences in the direction of greater severity. [44]

To avoid this outcome, some reformers now advo-
cate a middle ground whereby community parole supervision is retained but the discretionary authority
to release prisoners is structured very closely. [45]
Champions of this approach argue that the release
decisions will thereby become fairer, and that the
risk of lengthier and more costly prison sentences
in lieu of parole supervision will be averted.

SUMMARY

The future of parole in New York State is uncertain.
Both discretionary parole release authority and community parole supervision have come under severe
criticism in recent years, and their abolition or
reform has become one of the central issues in the
current national debate regarding sentencing policy
and practice. How the debate is resolved has enormous fiscal implications, not so much because of the
direct cost of parole but rather because of the way
parole affects the cost of imprisonment.

During fiscal 1978 New York taxpayers spent approximately $21 million for parole activities; about two-thirds of that sum was paid for supervision in home communities, and the remaining third was spent on the administration and Parole Board decision making. From a fiscal point of view, the more important impact of parole was on state prison costs. Had the State Parole Board required all those paroled during 1976 to serve another three months before being released, the prisons would have been forced to handle an estimated 1,100 additional convict-years of sentenced prisoners, enough to fill a medium-sized prison.

Even though prison costs are directly affected by parole decisions, the Parole Board maintains that the concerns of prison management are ignored in making release decisions. The outcome is an absence of effective control over these prison costs. To be sure, prison administrators do retain control over some cost factors in their domain, but the crucial decisions regulating admissions and releases remain outside their control.

Many reformers argue that the Parole Board's power to release prisoners be abolished, thereby requiring sentencing judges (or the legislatures) to fix the exact amount of time to be served behind bars. However, these reforms risk an enormous increase in spending for prisons, for the present-day political climate puts legislators and judges under great pressure to keep prisoners in for even longer periods than they now serve. During fiscal 1978 the average annual cost per state prisoner was $15,050 compared to an annual average of $1,090 for each parolee under supervision in the community. If parole supervision is eliminated or shortened while prison sentences become longer, the cost will be enormous. For example, had all those paroled in 1976 been required to serve their maximum sentences without parole (minus "good time"), the annual operating cost of the state prison system would have increased by $60 to $75 million. Building thousands of new prison cells would have been necessary, for the number of prisoners under custody at the end of 1976 would have increased approximately 25 percent.

A sensible reform of parole and sentencing practices must therefore address not only questions of fairness and equity, but also the management of prison populations and costs. Clarity and rationality in sentencing should not be achieved at the expense of longer sentences.

4
Probation

Judges in New York State have essentially two choices of "correctional programs" for convicted criminals: imprisonment or probation. Imprisonment re-
moves offenders from society, whereas a probation
sentence allows them to remain in the community under the supervision of the local probation department. Not only is probation a milder sanction than
imprisonment; it is also less costly. It is difficult to determine exactly how much less it costs
because there exists no accounting system which tal-
lies the total expenditures of all local government
probation departments. In New York City, however,
it cost an estimated average of $260 to $285 in fiscal 1978 to supervise a single probationer for a
year. This expenditure is infinitesimal compared
with the $15,000 spent to house one state prisoner
for a year.

The effectiveness of probation in New York has
not been thoroughly evaluated, but studies of other
jurisdictions indicate that probation is no less effective than imprisonment in preventing recidivism.[1]
Indeed, one analysis found that probation produced
better results than imprisonment for first offenders.[2] This suggests that expanding the use of probation for certain offenders might reap large savings at little additional risk to the community.

Despite its being the less expensive option,
probation is less frequently used as a sentencing
alternative than it was in the early 1970s. In 1974
46.3 percent of all persons indicted for felonies
and sentenced in the state superior courts received
probation, while 45.7 percent were imprisoned. By
1978 the proportion receiving probation slid to 32.4
percent, and 59.7 percent were imprisoned.[3] The
shift was most precipitous during 1974, probably as
a result of the 1973 penal law revisions which man-

71

dated prison terms for drug law offenders as well
as repeat felony offenders.

The probation caseload is still the largest of
any corrections program in the state, however. During 1977 there were more adults serving probation
sentences than all other sentences combined. At the
end of that year there were almost 55,000 adult probationers under supervision, whereas state prisons
held approximately 19,400 persons, parole had
13,500, and local jails held 3,700 sentenced prisoners.[4] Probation services across the state cost the
taxpayer an estimated $63 to $78 million in fiscal
1978. This represented about 10 to 13 percent of
the state's total corrections expenditure.

Probation has been called the "brightest hope
for corrections,"[5] but it is today a troubled institution. The National Advisory Commission on
Criminal Justice Standards and Goals assessed the
nationwide situation in words which aptly describe
probation in New York:

> Probation is not adequately structured,
> financed, staffed, or equipped with ne-
> cessary resources. A major shift of money
> and manpower to community-based corrections
> is necessary if probation is to be adopted
> nationally as the preferred disposition,
> as this Commission recommends. The shift
> will require strengthening the position of
> probation in the framework of government,
> defining goals and objectives for the pro-
> bation system, and developing an organiza-
> tion that can meet the goals and objectives.[6]

Probation lacks a clarity of purpose, a confu-
sion which stems in large part from the fact that
prisons have long dominated our discussion of the
criminal sanction. Probation has often been defined
as simply being "not prison." Stating what it is
not has hindered a clear definition of what it should
be. A myriad of community-based corrections programs has been gathered under the umbrella of the
probation department.

This chapter

- briefly reviews the organizational structure
  of probation in New York State;
- estimates the statewide cost of these
  services;
- examines in greater detail the cost and
  character of different probation services

in the state's largest local agency, the New
York City Department of Probation;
- reviews some proposals for strengthening probation; and
- discusses the efectiveness of probation as an
  alternative to imprisonment.

The Organization of Probation Services

Probation began as the "social work arm" of county
and municipal courts, and it continues to be a local
service.
  Throughout most of the state, probation agencies
are run by the counties. New York City is an exception to the pattern, having consolidated its five
county departments in a single metropolitan agency
in 1974. Three other rural counties (Warren, Fulton, and Montgomery) requested that their probation
departments be taken over by the state because they
were not able to maintain adequate services. At the
state government level, the small Division of Probation exercises general supervision of the local departments and assists in their financing, as well as
directly operating the departments in the three rural counties.
  Although their original mission was supervising
and assisting offenders in the community, probation
departments now support a wide range of social services. These include:

- court-ordered investigations of defendants
  awaiting sentencing and, less frequently,
  awaiting bail hearings;
- supervision of several categories of adju-
  dicated offenders (adult misdemeanants and
  felons, children in need of supervision,
  juvenile delinquents, juvenile offenders,
  and youthful offenders), and also of persons who fail to support their families;
- operating intake units in family courts;
- collection and disbursement of fines, restitution, and family support payments; and
- adoption investigations and marital
  counseling.

During 1977 more than 121,000 investigations

were completed for the courts, both adult criminal and family.[7] Over $119 million in court-ordered payments, primarily for family support but also for fines and restitution, was collected by all probation departments in the state.[8] (Restitution payments are turned over to the victims, and support payments to the families.)

Total Expenditures for Probation in New York State

Estimating the total costs of probation in New York's dispersed system is extremely hazardous because sufficient information is lacking. Even though the division has been discussing state take-over of all local departments for several years, it has no fiscal monitoring system that regularly reports how much money the statewide system costs. The division's chief finance officer reports that past requests to county departments have been unsuccessful in producing comparable data.[9]

The only available indicator of the total aggregated cost of probation in New York is the amount of state aid paid by the Division of Probation to local departments. This amount is a very weak estimator of total costs, however. Only certain costs are eligible for state reimbursement and there currently is no precise information which enables us to determine the ratio of reimbursable to total costs in all county departments.*

---

*The state currently pays 42.5% of all *reimbursable* expenses by local departments. The costs which are not eligible for partial reimbursement include capital outlay, debt service for capital improvements, fringe benefits, office and equipment rental and maintenance, insurance, utilities, indirect costs, transportation and inter- and intrastate transfer cases, witness fees, as well as some other costs. Moreover, *all* costs which are paid with federal funds are not reimbursable. Our own calculations show that only 26.5% of New York City's total probation costs were reimbursed by state aid during fiscal year 1978, 21.7% in Rockland County during 1977, 17.8% in Rensselaer, and 38.1% in Westchester. Therefore, it seems reasonable to estimate that the average subsidy rate outside New York City is between 25-35% of the total probation expenditures. The State Division estimates that about 31% of all budgeted 1979 probation costs are reimbursed by state aid monies.[10]

On the basis of our own data, however, we can make an estimate of the total aggregated *direct* cost of probation in our state. Firm expenditure data were obtained for the State Division of Probation and the largest of the local departments, New York City's. For all departments outside New York City, two figures are extrapolated from the $12.9 million paid out to these counties in state aid. It is probable that state aid pays between 25 and 35 percent of all direct probation costs in the counties. If the estimate of 35 percent is correct, the total cost of all direct expenditures for probation in fiscal 1978 was approximately $63 million. If state aid paid 25 percent of the total costs, the aggregate expenditure was about $78 million.

TABLE 4.1
Estimated Total Direct Expenditures
for Probation in New York State, 1978
(state and local agencies combined)[a]

NYS Division of Probation[b]	$ 2,629,795	
NYC Department of Probation	23,912,259	
Non-NYC County Departments	36,845,988[c]	to 51,584,384[d]
	$63,388,042	$78,126,438

Sources: New York State and counties from Appropriation Ledger Abstract, Form L-1 (dated 9/15/78), Division of Probation; New York City Department of Probation

[a]County and New York State figures are for New York State fiscal year 1978. No attempt was made to reconcile overlapping dates.
[b]Expenditures for state aid not included; they have been considered expenditures by local departments.
[c]Assumes 25:100 ratio of reimbursement to total direct cost.
[d]Assumes 35:100 ratio of reimbursement to total direct cost.

The Cost of Local Probation Services:
The New York City Example

To determine the cost of each type of probation
service, the expenditures of four probation departments throughout the state were examined. In all
but one, the costs of each separate service could
not be determined because these probation agencies
are not diversified enough to assign different costs
to each service. For example, the same probation
officer might conduct an investigation for all
courts -- adult and family -- and might also occa-
sionally supervise an offender placed on probation.
Lacking a detailed survey of how each officer spends
his or her time, it was impossible to even estimate
the different costs with any accuracy.

New York City's Department of Probation, on the
other hand, is marked by a functional division of
labor which makes cost analysis possible. This a-
gency is probably the largest locally operated probation department in the country, having twenty-
four branches throughout the city. These different
branches specialize in a single type of service, and
expenditures for most can be distinguished. Table
4.2 estimates how the department spent its resources
in fiscal 1978. [11]

By far the largest effort of the department is
the servicing of New York City's adult courts, both
supreme and criminal. An estimated $14 million, or
58.6 percent of total expenditures in fiscal 1978,
was for these services. About half of this $14 mil-
lion was spent on presentence investigation of offenders for the courts. The other half was spent on
supervising adults sentenced to probation.

Approximately 36 percent of department expenditures in fiscal 1978 went for family court services,
including intake, investigation, supervision, and
the alternatives to detention program. (This latter
service "diverts" youths who have been brought into
the family courts, places them in day-care facilities, and provides them with intensive services.)
First year supervision costs include the cost of intake, investigation, and supervision. Second year
supervision is less costly since intake and investigation are not repeated.

Adult Court Investigations: In both the superior
and lower courts (or supreme and criminal in New
York City), all persons who have been convicted of
crimes that call for imprisonment for ninety days or
more must be investigated by the local probation

TABLE 4.2
Expenditures by Function:
New York City Department of Probation, FY 1978

	Estimated Costs per Unit of Activity	Total Cost of Service, Including Estimated Fringe and Pension Costs
Executive Management	---	$1,188,414 (4.9%)
Family Court Services[a]		
Intake	$70/interview	$3,089,874
Investigation	$681/investigation	2,852,192
Supervision	$1,275/youth/year	2,139,143
Alternatives to Detention	$5,527/youth/year[b]	475,365
		$8,556,574 (35.8%)
Adult Court Services		
Investigations		$ 6,892,794
Supreme Court	$343/investigation	
Criminal Court	$141/investigation	
Supervision		7,130,477
Supreme Court	$260/probationer/year	
Criminal Court	$285/probationer/year	
		$14,023,271 (58.6%)
Undistributed Other-than-Personal Services Expenditures		$ 144,000 (0.6%)
		$23,912,259 (100%)

Source: Computed from data supplied by New York City Department of Probation

[a]These functional costs *include* expenditures for Family Court Liaison officers who provide a variety of general overhead services.
[b]The Dept. of Probation notes that this overestimates the actual cost per youth because several hundred children voluntarily attend who are not officially counted in the *Mayor's Management Report,* the source of program data for this function.

department prior to sentencing. This is because
judges are obliged by the current sentencing laws to
tailor a sentence to the perceived rehabilitative
needs of the offender and to balance these needs
against the demand for public safety. Although
judges already have sketchy information about the
offense and the offender's prior criminal record,
they usually know little of the individual's social
background. Probation officers are charged with the
task of compiling a social and criminal history of
the individual (and sometimes a psychological history or examination if ordered by the court), and
this information is compressed into a report sent
to the judge. The reports evaluate the offenders'
fitness for probation and recommend what type of
sentence seems appropriate. These recommendations
are approved by department supervisors and appended
to the reports submitted to the sentencing judges.

During fiscal 1978, 17,679 investigations were
completed for the Criminal Courts in New York City
at an estimated cost of $141 each.[12] Another 12,873
were done for the Supreme Courts, costing an estimated $343 apiece.[13] Comparatively more money was
spent on Supreme Court investigations because the
cases brought before the Supreme Courts are more
serious and face heavier penalties. Moreover, defendants in Supreme Court cases are more likely to
be in detention while awaiting sentence. Because
the daily operating cost of jailing one prisoner in
New York City averaged $68 during fiscal 1978, money
spent to speed investigations contributes to larger
savings in the Department of Correction accounts.
(As will be discussed in Chapter 6, the average cost
of *detention* was even higher than $68.)

Sentences to Probation Supervision: During fiscal
1978 approximately 40 percent of the state's entire
probation caseload was carried by the New York City
Department of Probation. At any one time, there
were approximately 10,000 persons on probation under
orders from the New York City Criminal Courts, and
another 16,500 from Supreme Courts.[14] The estimated
annual cost in New York City of supervising one
adult probationer sentenced by the Supreme Court was
$260 during fiscal 1978. The estimated cost of su-
pervising Criminal Court cases was slightly higher,
$285.*

---

*The cost of supervision is generally lower in New
York City than in other parts of the state because

The purpose of this supervision is to protect the public by assisting "probationers to comply with conditions of probation so as to prevent recidivism." [16] The specific conditions are imposed upon the offenders at time of sentencing. They might include a requirement that the probationer attend school, be employed, support his or her dependents, receive therapy at a local clinic, or make restitution to the victim of the crime. Narcotics offenders often have special conditions placed upon them by the courts, including participation in a treatment program. Alcohol abusers sometimes have similar restrictions placed upon them. Common to all is the requirement that the probationer report regularly to his or her probation officer. Probation officers are required to monitor probationers to see that the conditions are being fulfilled. If compliance is lacking, the officer can bring the offender back into court for resentencing to jail or prison.

Even though the law authorizes a probation sentence when institutional confinement is "not necessary for the protection of the public," [17] some judges seem to think that public protection requires a probation sentence to be coupled with a short jail term. The intention appears to be an attempt to deter the lawbreaker from future crimes. The use of this practice (called "shock probation" or "split sentencing") somewhat confuses the purposes of probation. One commentator has noted that "whatever merit may inhere in this taste of jail idea, it does muddy the sentencing structure's underlying philosophy that if, in a given case, a term of imprisonment is not appropriate, it should not be imposed." [18]

Inadequate Resources for Probation Supervision: In handling a case over to the probation officer, the

---

the city department has been badly hit by budget cuts. Between January 1, 1975 and June 1, 1977 the number of employees in the department declined by 25%, and the major losses were suffered in the branches responsible for supervising probationers. This resulted in an enlarged caseload for each probation officer, reducing the per case cost. In Delaware County's small probation department, the cost of one year's supervision during 1979 was estimated to be $234 for "special" cases requiring at least one contact per month, $446 for "active" cases involving twice as many contacts, and $918 for "intensive" weekly contact. [15]

courts are clearly requiring that the probationer
receive individual attention and assistance. What
that attention consists of and how effective it is
has been the subject of very little systematic evaluation. Examining the most superficial information,
however, shows that New York City's Department of
Probation is too understaffed to provide comprehensive services to all those consigned to its custody.
During fiscal 1978 the department assigned an average of 129 probationers to each officer servicing
the Supreme Court. The average caseload in Criminal
Court Branch was 126 probationers.[19]

Probation officers cannot perform more than
minimal surveillance or assistance with this many
"clients." With a 35-hour work week, an average
caseload of 126 to 129 means that only 55 minutes
per month of the officer's time is available to each
probationer.[20]

In response to this lack of sufficient resources, probation officers informally adjust their
schedules so that those offenders needing more services or surveillance receive more attention, leaving
those less difficult cases with little more than
routine checking-in.[21] The State Division of Probation has articulated a standard that agencies do
this formally, providing a "system of differential
supervision based on the program needs of all probationers."[22] There exist few devices to systema-
tically assess and compare the needs of a probationer as well as the offender's potential risk to the
community, however. The New York City department is
in the process of developing procedures to evaluate
risk and need, and will then be able to formally
categorize its probationers into four different
classes, each requiring varying frequencies of
"contact."[23]

Of the 55 minutes of an officer's time poten-
tially available to each probationer, much of it is
spent not on counseling but rather on law-enforce-
ment or other administrative tasks. A 1977 Economic Development Commission study noted: "Much Probation Officer activity consists of following up on
re-arrest notices (the 'hit list') in notifying the
court, in eventual filing of violation petitions,
and in preparing progress reports as requested by
the court.... Substantial time is spent on filing
for early discharge of probationers."[24]

Given the sheer weight of numbers, it is not
surprising that officers spend little time in the
probationers' home communities. The same EDC report
states: "Home visits are infrequent or non-existent.

Most contacts consist of reporting to the branch
headquarters, on a monthly basis or even less frequently."[25]   The location of these branch headquarters far from where most probationers live further
discourages home visiting.

Probation officers are not aided by a strong
supportive staff. The clerical staff of the supervision branches suffered most from budget cuts, and
in fiscal 1978 there was only one full-time clerk
employed by the department for every *five* probation
officers.[26] The department has begun to contract out
some work to the private sector, but probation officers do more of their own paperwork now.*

Strengthening Probation Services

Developing formalized procedures for differential
supervision might help the probation department better "target" its scarce resources, but there are
other alternatives for augmenting the manpower
available for assisting the probationer. These include the expanded use of volunteers, the trans-
formation of the probation officer's role into a
community resource broker, handing the job of presentence investigation over to the courts, and restructuring the funding of probation so that the
state assumes a greater share of the cost. Closer
evaluation of all these alternatives is needed to
determine their cost-effectiveness.

Volunteers for probation: Several probation agencies across the country have enlisted the help of
volunteers. Indeed, probation began as a service
provided by volunteers. The New York City department has successfully used volunteers, but only in
a limited way. The volunteer organizations have included the American Red Cross, the National Council
of Jewish Women, the AFL-CIO, Alcoholics Anonymous,

---

*Caseload and clerical support staff patterns ex-
plain much of the difference between the cost of
probation and parole supervision. As noted in Chapter 3, it cost an average of $1,090 to supervise a
single parolee for one year during fiscal 1978, about
four times the cost per probationer. The average
parole caseload per officer was about 50 during the
same period that each probation officer had almost
120 probationers. Whereas five probation officers
had to share a single clerk, there were approximate-
two clerks per parole officer in fiscal 1978.

and various colleges and universities. The EDC report noted that the volunteer program is "impressive but very small." Some branch officers used no volunteers, and others used them for relatively short periods of time.[27] Expanding the use of volunteers should be explored as a means of relieving the burden on probation officers.

Community resource managers: Another strategy for expanding the resources available for probation assistance is to transform the probation officer into a broker for services already provided by outside agencies. Probation supervision has traditionally been dominated by the casework approach, which assigns the officer the sole responsibility for treating the client. The National Advisory Commission on Criminal Justice Standards and Goals finds that this approach "no longer meets the needs of the criminal justice system, the probation system, or the offender." The commission notes: "While some probation officers still will have to carry out counseling duties, most probation officers can meet the goals of the probation services system more effectively in the role of community resource manager. This means that the probation officer will have primary responsibility for meshing a probationer's identified needs with a range of available services and for supervising the delivery of those services."[28] This model of probation supervision has been experimented with in some western states but has not yet been definitively evaluated.

In line with this is the proposal that probation officers should actively advise sentencing judges about the availability of community services.[29] Presentence reports submitted to the courts seldom identify specific agencies in the community able to provide the needed service. Were this to be done more frequently, it might be possible for sentencing judges to expand their use of alternatives to incarceration.

Several proposals for providing higher quality probation supervision have focused on the broader restructuring of probation agencies. These include shedding activities which are not related to the agencies' primary criminal justice mission, transferring the responsibility for court-ordered investigations to the courts, and a greater assumption of fiscal and/or management responsibility by the state government.

Severing investigations from supervision: In New York

City the capacity to supervise and assist probationers has been weakened by severe cutbacks in funding.
As discussed above, a delay in finishing court-
ordered investigations often results in increased
costs of incarceration because many defendants
await sentencing in jail.

It has been argued that giving the responsibility for investigations to the courts will protect
the resources given to supervision. This indeed
would relieve probation administrators from having
to choose between spending on investigations and
supervision, but this allocation decision would
simply be shifted to a higher level. There is no
guarantee that the Mayor's Office in New York City
or his Office of Management and Budget would provide
the department with adequate funds for an expanded
supervision capability.

A state takeover of probation: One controversial
proposal to strengthen probation is the recommendation that the state government assume greater fiscal
and management responsibility for probation services.[30] One sector of the criminal justice system --
the courts -- is already going this route. Transferring the responsibility from the local government
to the state is seen by its proponents as the best
solution to the chronic underfinancing of probation.

Unlike the prison and parole systems, probation
in New York is marked by wide disparities in service
from one county to another. The root of this dis-
parity is the dependence of probation agencies on
local revenues. New York counties vary greatly in
the size of their tax bases, and this variation in
turn results in an uneven availability of services.
Probation caseloads have been rising for over a decade, but many local governments have become increasingly strained as their revenues cannot keep pace
with demands for services.

To help local governments pay for probation
services, the State Division of Probation transfers
millions of dollars to locally operated departments.
As Table 4.3 shows, over $19 million was trans-
ferred to localities by the state government for
probation assistance in fiscal 1978.

The costs of probation have increased greatly
during the past two decades, and the amount of state
subsidies has also increased enormously. From fiscal 1961 to 1976 state aid to local probation increased *fortyfold*. The decline in reimbursement since
1976 reflects the recent budget cuts in many local
probation departments, especially in New York City.

TABLE 4.3
State Aid to Local Probation, FY 1961-78

State Fiscal Year Ending In	Amount	State Fiscal Year Ending In	Amount
1961	$ 583,931	1970	$12,746,802
1962	924,660	1971	14,191,979
1963	1,351,663	1972	17,237,225
1964	2,395,756	1973	17,384,111
1965	2,988,557	1974	18,249,672
1966	5,224,943	1975	15,369,702
1967	9,745,374	1976	25,594,915
1968	10,396,836	1977	21,043,882
1969	11,970,073	1978	19,343,540

Sources: 1961-1977 data: State Aid to Local Government, 1977 New York State Department of Audit and Control, Division of Municipal Affairs, Bureau of Municipal Research and Statistics (Dec. 1977), p. 138. 1978 data: Appropriation Ledger Abstract, Form L-1, dated 9/15/78, New York State Division of Probation.

This transfer does not completely relieve the fiscal pressure on local probation departments, however, for it provides only partial reimbursement of costs. As discussed earlier, the state subsidy probably covers no more than 25 to 35 percent of the total costs. In one of the counties examined for this report, the state subsidy reimbursed only 17.8 percent of the total annual probation costs.

For several years the State Division of Probation has been discussing proposals for full state financing. This has usually been coupled with a proposal to assume full management duties. The model for this is the "direct service" now provided Fulton, Warren, and Montgomery counties by the state division.[31]

Some of the poorer counties are reported to be interested in this arrangement because of the savings to local budgets. At present the Mayor's Office in New York City is thinking about requesting the state to take over the burden of probation. Other more affluent county departments oppose such a

move, however, because they fear that the state
would bleed some of their resources away to pay for
expanded services in the poorer counties. Equalization is likely to bring the richer departments
down to some median level rather than bring all departments up to the level of the most affluent.
This strategy thus appears to work to the advantage
of the poor counties and to the disadvantage of the
wealthier ones. Others also object to moving away
from community-controlled probation services. It is
felt that a more removed state-level administration
would be less responsive to the unique needs of each
local community.

One alternative proposal which deserves consideration is the expansion of the state aid program
without direct control by the State Division of Probation. This might alleviate the difficulties inherent in relying on local revenues without sacri-
ficing the advantages of decentralized community-
based control. One model is that of the Minnesota
state subsidy, which assists local communities
demonstrating a greater need at a higher rate of
state aid. The Minnesota plan intends to achieve a
greater parity in correctional service delivery a-
mong the counties, and the subsidy rate is determined by a complex equalization formula which bal-
ances local need with ability to pay. Need and
ability are measured by per capita income, per capita taxable value, per capita expenditures for correctional purposes, and percent of county population between the ages of six and thirty.[32] The advantage of this kind of arrangement is that local
control of probation would be continued while relieving the revenue crisis felt by local administrators.

Yet another possibility is to enlist the subsidy payments in the service of a broader objective,
such as the reduction of state prison admissions.
The earliest program of this sort was the California
Probation Subsidy, begun in 1965.[33] The legislature
desired to reduce the burden on the state prison
system (and on the state budget), and a series of
incentives was designed to encourage keeping convicted offenders in the home counties rather than
sending them to prison. To provide localities with
monies to improve probation supervision, the state
government recompensed the localities for each convicted offender *not* sent to state prison.

The Probation Subsidy has been credited with
producing a dramatic drop in admissions to state
prisons. Between 1965 and 1974 it was estimated

that approximately 40,000 first admissions to state prisons were averted as a consequence of the subsidy program, generating a savings to the state of at least $19 million.[34] Another evaluation suggests that the prisoner population declined for other reasons, and that local jail admissions might have increased, which merely changed the location of commitment rather than the balance between incarceration and probation.[35] Forecasting the impact of a similar subsidy in New York requires rigorous examination.

The Effectiveness of Probation as a Sentencing Alternative

Sentencing convicted offenders to probation instead of prison not only entails a lower direct cost to the taxpayer, but there is evidence that it is as effective as imprisonment in reducing recidivism. Indeed, some evidence indicates that for first offenders, probation sentences are more likely than imprisonment to yield crime-control benefits.

A 1970 study of California sentencing and recidivism patterns found that probationers were more likely to avoid arrest for a new crime or technical violation of probation/parole during a one-year follow-up period than persons who had been incarcerated and released. This difference persists even when the type of offense, prior record, age, sex, and county are taken into account.[36] Two English studies reached similar conclusions.[37]

The findings of a study in Wisconsin "clearly indicate that for first offenders, probation is superior to imprisonment (plus parole)." For those offenders with prior records, there was no difference in rate of reconviction for new offenses or technical violations.[38] More research needs to be done. However, it is clear that large numbers of offenders could be given probation sentences instead of prison without significant decrease in public safety.

SUMMARY

A sentence to probation under supervision in the community rather than incarceration is considerably less expensive than either a prison or jail term. Further, there is evidence that it is no less effective than incarceration in preventing recidivism. Some studies show that first offenders placed on probation are even less likely to commit future crimes than similar persons released from jail or prison.

During 1977-78 annual spending for probation amounted to an estimated $63 to $78 million. A more precise determination of total costs is impossible given the state of the current reporting systems. Unlike prisons and parole, probation departments are agencies of local governments except in three small counties, where the State Division of Probation directly operates the agencies. No central organization, including the Division of Probation, collects accurate information on all probation costs at the local level.*

Determining the precise cost of probation supervision in a single local agency is also impossible because the accounting systems in most departments do not separate the expenditures for each of the different probation services. (Probation departments offer a wide range of other services, including, for example, investigating persons awaiting sentencing, assisting the Family Court, collecting support payments and the like.) Only in New York City could expenditures for probation supervision be distinguished from other costs. During fiscal 1978 taxpayers spent an estimated average of $260 and $285 respectively to supervise for one year a single probationer sentenced by Criminal and Supreme Courts. Presentence investigations cost an estimated $141 and $343 each.

New York City probation costs are generally lower than elsewhere in the state because the agency budget was severely cut during the recent fiscal crisis. Case loads have soared to the point where each probation officer supervised an average of 126

---

*As this report was going to the printer the Division of Probation completed a survey of statewide probation budgets for fiscal 1979.

to 129 offenders at any one time during fiscal
1978. This meant that only 55 minutes per month
of the officers' time were available for each probationer. Probation was about four times less
costly per supervision case than parole during the
same period, largely because parole officers had
smaller caseloads and more clerical support staff.

The Executive Law authorizes the state government to provide financial assistance to local probation departments so that services can meet minimum standards of sufficiency. Determining the ratio
of state aid to total local costs could not be done
because those total local costs could not be established. However, an examination of four probation
departments found that the rate of state subsidy
ranged from 17.8 to 38.1 percent. On the basis of
this sample, it is estimated that the state pays
only 25 to 35 percent of all local probation costs.

Most local governments in New York are hard-
pressed for sufficient revenues, and the state subsidy is not large enough to ensure an evenly adequate level of service throughout all localities.
Strategies for expanding the resources available to
probation include an increased use of volunteers,
more frequent referrals to public and private service agencies, a stronger state subsidy program, and
a complete assumption of probation costs by the
state government. The last proposal has receieved
much attention during the past several years, but it
is not yet clear how administrative responsibility
might be shared by local and state agencies.

5
Local Jails and Penitentiaries

In addition to the $285.5 million spent on state
prisons, New Yorkers paid an estimated $240 million
to operate local jails and penitentiaries during
1977-1978.* The average cost of holding a prisoner
in these facilities ranged from approximately
$14,065 to $24,855 per year, or $38.50 to $68 per
day, depending upon the county.

    Two types of persons are held in these local
institutions: those awaiting determination of guilt
or innocence, and those sentenced to terms of less
than a year for committing lesser crimes (misdemeanors, violations, or lesser felonies).

    Like state prison officials, jail administra-
tors cannot effectively control all the factors
which affect local corrections costs. The decision
to admit arrested persons is made by the police and
the courts. The decision to release them is made by
the courts and often by the bail bondsmen who establish the collateral which defendants or their repre-
sentatives must post in order to make bail. In the
case of sentenced prisoners, the decision to release
is made by the judge (by virtue of setting a sentence to be served) or by the parole board, which
has the authority to parole prisoners serving more
than ninety days in a local facility.

    Holding local corrections costs down therefore
requires a coordinated effort by many agencies. To
date, these efforts have generally occurred only
when the jails are severely overcrowded. The fact

---

*Because New York City's fiscal year does not match
county accounting periods, this $237.3 million is a
composite of spending for New York City jails during
fiscal 1978 and expenditures by counties for jails
and penitentiaries during calendar year 1977.

that these strategies substantially reduce prisoner populations indicates that a more sustained effort could produce a long-term reduction in jail use. Cost-controlling policies of these sorts are especially necessary as local governments become increasingly strapped for revenues.

This chapter

- describes the character of local corrections;
- estimates the cost of jailing in New York State;
- examines in detail jail costs in three counties;
- analyzes why jail costs differ from one county to another; and
- describes several strategies for reducing jail costs, including diverting pretrial defendants from detention, creating alternatives to money bail, and broader use by police of court summonses instead of physical arrests.

The Character of Local Corrections

Local governments in New York finance and operate three types of facilities for holding persons in custody: lock-ups, jails, and penitentiaries.

The first stop after arrest is generally a lock-up or jail operated by a city, town or village.* There are over over 200 of these holding places outside New York City,[1] and during 1977 85,750 cases were admitted to them.[2] The cost of these dispersed facilities was not determined, for no central agency collects this fiscal information. Many of the holding pens in New York City are run by the municipal Department of Correction, and its records show more than a quarter of a million admissions during 1977.[3] The cost of these pens was not isolated from the more general cost of jailing in New York City, which is discussed in Chapter 6.

After being charged and arraigned before a judge, defendants who remain in custody are trans-

*In some small counties, arrested persons are taken directly to jails run by the counties.

ferred from a municipal lock-up to the local county jail.* There exist fifty-seven of these jails outside New York City, and they admitted 94,963 cases during 1977.[5] Most of these jails are small and old. Only ten have more than 200 cells. A third were built over fifty years ago and ten in the nineteenth century; only 42 percent of the jail cells in New York State were built after World War II. Jails are administered by the county sheriffs, except in Westchester and New York City, where the jails are run by a separate Department of Correction headed by a commissioner.

Many persons detained in the local jails spend only a few hours or days before being released on their own recognizance, while others are detained awaiting trial for many months. During 1977 the average pretrial detention period in these facilities was two weeks.[6] On the last day of 1977, there were 1,820 persons awaiting trial in these fifty-seven county jails.[7] In New York City the burden was much heavier; during December of that year there was an average of 4,231 arraigned persons in custody awaiting trial.[8]

As mentioned, jails also hold persons convicted and sentenced to terms of less than a year. During 1976 these jails admitted 18,600 sentenced persons.** New York City admitted over 18,000 cases during 1977.[9]

In four counties (Erie, Westchester, Albany, and Onondaga), sentenced prisoners are not sent to the county jails but rather to the local penitentiary. During 1977 there were 3,690 admissions to these institutions.[10] Like the county jails, the penitentiaries are operated and fully funded by the local county governments. Responsibility for their operation rests with the sheriffs, or the Commissioner of Correction in Westchester.

In far too many jurisdictions the quality of the jails can only be called abysmal. Indeed, the courts are increasingly finding jails in violation of the Eighth Amendment prohibition of "cruel and unusual punishment." Government "watchdog" agencies such as the State Commission of Correction and the

---

*New York City has no county-financed jails, for they were consolidated into a single municipal system. In 1977, 55,000 persons were returned to custody after arraignment for continued pretrial detention.[4]
**1977 data for county jails is incomplete.

New York City Board of Correction are beginning to establish minimum standards but compliance with them has often been slow. According to the assessment of Chief Judge Kaufman of the U.S. Court of Appeals, Second Circuit:

> When the history of our criminal justice system is chronicled, no doubt one of its most sobering pages will describe the sad state of this nation's prisons and jails. Whether it be filthy, narrow cells of an Alabama penitentiary or in overcrowded dormitories in a Bronx house of detention, we have quartered individuals, both convicted or merely accused of crimes, major and minor, under conditions that shock the conscience of civilized men.[11]

The irony of this is that we generally provide more amenities to persons convicted of serious crimes and banished to state prisons. Almost all persons placed in local jails, including those charged with traffic violations, are routinely placed in maximum-security cells. Clothing is generally not provided even though one might have to wait months before coming to trial. Although state prisoners are permitted "contact visits" (in which prisoners are allowed to hold hands with family and friends across a table), prisoners and visitors in forty-seven of the county jails are crowded into small booths where they see each other through a narrow pane of glass, and communicate by telephones.* Jail prisoners in many counties are provided very few therapeutic, educational, or recreational programs. This stems in part from the lack of a clear mandate to provide programs in most areas. Most people in jail are awaiting trial and have not been sentenced to a period of "treatment," as state prisoners have.

---

*In a case decided in March 1979, the Second Circuit Court of Appeals ruled again that contact visiting is a constitutional right for pretrial detainees, and that plans must be made to provide them in all jails. *Macera v. Chinlund*, 595 F. 2d 1231 (2d Cir., 1979).

The Cost of Jailing in New York State

Determining the cost of operating jails throughout
the state is difficult due to the fragmented character of fiscal responsibility. As noted above, there
is no information available about those most dispersed holding places, the municipal lock-ups. For
county jails and penitentiaries, the only source of
1977 data is the State Commission of Correction.
This agency aggregates expenditure reports from the
county sheriffs (or corrections commissioners where
they exist). These reports are imperfect indicators
of costs, but they provide the information upon
which reasonable estimates can be based.* More detailed costs for the New York City Department of
Correction are presented in Chapter 6.

Table 5.1 shows that the estimated total cost
of local corrections, including New York City's, was
$240.2 million in fiscal 1978.**

During 1977 the county jails housed a daily average of 3,968 prisoners [12] at an estimated daily
cost of $38.50 each, or $14,065 per year. The penitentiaries held an average of 575 sentenced prisoners each day [13] at a substantially higher cost. During the same year, the average daily cost of keeping
a single prisoner in these four institutions was
$63.05, or approximately $23,013 per year. The cost
of jailing in New York City was still higher: during fiscal 1978 the average cost per prisoner was
$68 per day, or $24,855 annually.

Jail Costs in Three Counties

The expenditure information made available to us was
not detailed enough to demonstrate the differences

---

*The sheriffs' reports include some nonjail costs
(highway patrol) and exclude some costs borne by
other government agencies, such as fringe benefits,
retirement contributions, utilities in some counties, and undoubtedly many other indirect costs. We
have estimated fringe and retirement fund contributions to be 30 percent of gross salary, and have added these into the Table 5.1 totals. There is no
way to estimate the size of the nonjail costs, so no
adjustment was made to exclude them.
**New York City data reflect fiscal 1978 expendi-
tures; the county data are for calendar year 1977.

94

TABLE 5.1
Cost of Operating Local Jails and Penitentiaries, 1977-1978

New York City (FY 1978)

Salaries	$ 68,175,301	
Salary Adjustments	10,168,126	
Fringe Benefits	21,575,265	
Retirement Contributions	27,527,895	
Other Than Personal Services	18,510,000	
Outside Services	25,221,000	
		$171,177,587 (71%)

County Jails Outside New York City (1977)

Chief Administrator Salaries	$ 1,101,984	
Employee Salaries	30,743,461	
Estimated Fringe and Pension	9,553,634	
Inmate Meals	4,042,648	
Utilities	1,517,577	
Plant Improvements	2,891,615	
Maintenance	24,580	
Miscellaneous Other	5,942,558	
		$ 55,818,057 (23%)

County Penitentiaries Outside
New York City (1977)

Chief Administrator Salaries	$ 106,362	
Employee Salaries	6,678,053	
Estimated Fringe and Pension	2,035,325	
Inmate Meals	964,099	
Utilities	441,630	
Plant Improvements	62,914	
Maintenance	2,104,269	
Miscellaneous Other	840,030	
		$ 13,232,682 (6%)

$240,228,326

Sources: See Chapter 6 for New York City data.
County costs provided by New York State Commission
of Correction, letters dated 7/18/78 and 4/3/79;
estimated fringe and pension costs added.

in costs between jails and penitentiaries or the differences from one county to another. To better understand the variation in local correction costs, three county jails were visited: Rockland, Westchester, and Rensselaer. These counties were chosen as illustrative cases and they differ from each other in important ways, including the extent to which their populations are rural, suburban, or urban, per capital income, the size of their tax base, and the simplicity or complexity of their correctional systems.

The costs of jailing in the two county jails and the three facilities in Westchester are shown in tables 5.2 and 5.3. Corrections costs in Westchester are considerably higher than in the other two counties. In Rensselaer the daily cost per prisoner during 1977 was $47, or $17,200 a year. The cost in Rockland was $45 per inmate-day, or $16,400 a year. The combined average for all three Westchester facilities was $58 per inmate-day, or $21,000 per year.

Table 5.3 also indicates a large cost difference between jailing men and women in Westchester. Both the men's jail and penitentiary cost about the same per inmate-day, that is, about $56. The women's facility, however, cost $81 per day, or $29,700 per inmate-year.

Explaining the Different Costs

The cost of local jails and penitentiaries is determined by four broad factors: (1) administrative policies regarding staffing, salaries, productivity, and the kind and level of services to be offered; (2) ability of the local government to pay, which largely reflects the size of the local tax base; (3) the willingness of local government officials to spend their resources for jails as opposed to other services; and (4) the extent to which the local courts require imprisonment before trial and after conviction.

Administrative policies: Table 5.3 shows that much of the difference in costs is due to staffing and to spending for medical services. In both Rockland and Rensselaer approximately $28 per prisoner was spent daily on staff salaries plus adjustments, overtime, and differentials, while the women's facility in Westchester spent almost $49 per prisoner each day. This difference is partly explained by the total number of staff at these facilities, and also by the

TABLE 5.2
Cost of Adult Corrections in Three Counties, by Object, 1977
(in $1,000s)

	Rensselaer	Rockland	Westchester (with administrative costs distributed)		
			Men's Jail	Penitentiary	Women's Correctional Unit
Salaries	$474 (58%)	$ 631 (56%)	$2,141 (46%)	$2,149 (55%)	$540 (59%)
Benefits	145 (17)	191 (17)	841 (18)	844 (22)	212 (23)
Overtime, Adjustments, and Differentials	16 (2)	76 (7)	49 (1)	47 (1)	12 (1)
Food	50 (6)	51 (4)	206 (4)	167 (4)	28 (3)
Miscellaneous Supplies	16 (2)	17 (2)	59 (2)	68 (2)	6 (1)
Medical	57 (7)	94 (8)	1,071 (23)	225 (6)	49 (5)
Repairs & Maintenance	3 (0.4)	3 (0.2)	98 (2)	76 (2)	18 (2)
Equipment	7 (0.8)	3 (0.2)	14 (0.3)	15 (0.3)	2 (0.2)
Public Works	22 (3)	61 (5)	93 (2)	189 (5)	41 (4)
Inmate Payments	-0-	-0-	6 (0.1)	41 (1)	4 (0.4)
Law Department	-0-	-0-	7 (0.1)	3 (0.07)	1 (0.1)
Misc. Other Expenses	34 (4)	6 (1.5)	87 (2)	54 (1)	9 (1)
	$824 (100%)	$1,133 (100%)	$4,672 (100%)	$3,878 (100%)	$922 (100%)

Sources:
County Annual Reports, 1977, State of N.Y., Dept. of Audit & Control, Div. of Municipal Affairs

TABLE 5.3
Cost Per Inmate-Day in Three Counties, 1977

				Westchester	
					Women's
		Rock-	Men's	Peniten-	Correctional
	Rensselaer	land	Jail	tiary	Unit
Salaries	$27.05	$25.05	$25.73	$30.83	$47.72
Overtime, Adjustments, and Differentials	.91	3.02	.59	.67	1.06
Employee Benefits	8.28	7.58	10.10	12.11	18.74
Food	2.85	2.06	2.48	2.40	2.47
Other Materials and Supplies	.91	.68	.71	.98	.53
Medical	3.25	3.75	12.87	3.23	4.33
Repairs and Maintenance	.17	.12	1.18	1.09	1.59
Equipment	.40	.12	.17	.22	.17
Public Works	1.26	2.42	1.12	2.71	3.62
Miscellaneous Expenses	1.94	.24	1.20	.77	.80
Inmate Wages	-0-	-0-	.07	.59	.35
Law Department	-0-	-0-	.08	.04	.09
	$47.01	$45.04	$56.30	$55.64	$81.47

Sources: 1977 County Annual Reports

substantial differences in salary levels. (See Table 5.4).

TABLE 5.4
Average Salaries, 1977

Position	Rensselaer	Rockland	Westchester
Corrections Officer	$ 6,600	$10,238	$15,900
Senior Corrections Officer	7,100	12,300	(none)
Sergeants	7,700	(none)	19,200
Captains	10,000	(none)	22,000
Warden or equivalent	10,000	18,100	26,300-32,100

Westchester pays much more for health care in its correctional facilities. A new medical services wing operated by the county hospital was recently built and endowed with modern and expensive equipment. There is a psychiatric staff of fifteen and special living quarters for psychiatric in-patients. Their quarters have glass rather than bars, private baths, and sophisticated electronic monitoring and communications systems. As a result, daily expenditures for health services were $8.19 per prisoner in Westchester, compared with $3.25 in Rensselaer and $3.73 in Rockland.

The ability and willingness to pay for services: Local governments differ in their ability and willingness to support adequate jails and penitentiaries. As noted in Chapter 1, local governments derive a large part of their revenues from local sources such as the property and sales taxes. The simple consequence of this is that counties with larger tax bases have more money to spend on public services of all kinds.

Westchester County has the largest tax base of the three. One component of that tax base -- the per capita income of its residents -- was approximately $6,800 in 1974, compared with $5,300 in Rockland and $4,200 in Rensselaer.[14] Westchester also spent proportionately more of its monies on criminal justice and corrections. Nine percent of its total spending for operations was for criminal justice, and 3 percent of its criminal justice spending was for the county jails and penitentiaries. Rennselaer, the poorest of the county governments, spent approximately the same (8.6 percent) of its total revenues for criminal justice purposes, and less (2 percent) of its criminal justice money for the county jail. Rockland County, intermediate between the two in overall government spending, spent considerably less (5.5 percent of total operations) for criminal justice, and still less of its criminal justice money (1 percent) for the county jail.[15]

These different spending patterns are not a direct reflection of crime and arrest rates. Westchester does indeed have the highest crime rate of the three, but it was only 17 percent higher in 1977 than Rockland's, the lowest. The arrest rates among the three counties differed by 26 percent.[16] Spending for corrections differed by a much larger factor.

Similar comparisons could not be made for all counties in New York State. The general impression, however, is that jails are underfinanced, and this in large part is attributable to the fiscal strain on local governments coupled with the lack of political "clout" possessed by prisoners and their families. Although there are exceptions, the general picture of local government financing is one of too many demands and too few dollars. Local sources of revenue have not been able to generate enough money, both cities and counties have had to rely increasingly on aid from the state and federal governments. In 1975, for example, almost half of the revenues in counties outside New York City were transfers from these higher-level governments; 18 percent came from the state and 28 percent from the federal government.[17]

Many local government officials who are saddled with substandard jails argue that they cannot upgrade the quality of the jails because they do not have the money. Some states (Minnesota, California, Virginia, Arizona, Ohio, and Pennsylvania, for example) have developed programs of state aid earmarked for local corrections.[18] In general, two broad classes of programs exist in these states. Some have the expressed goal of achieving compliance with the minimum standards promulgated by the state and aid is contingent upon the local governments' meeting these standards. (The New York State proba-

tion subsidy program is ostensibly of this variety.)
Other programs aim at the equalization of correctional services throughout all local jurisdictions,
and the subsidy rate is therefore determined by a
complex formula assessing need, ability to pay, and
tax effort. The appropriateness of these state subsidy programs for local jails deserves close study
as they might provide New York with a model for improved local corrections.

County differences in jail use: The cost of local
jails reflects not only administrative policies and
the ability and willingness of the county to spend
for corrections, but it also depends on how heavily
the locality relies on its jails. There are significant differences in how the three counties used
their jails in 1977. Table 5.5 illustrates these
differences.

In Rensselaer 49 out of every 100 persons arrested are detained in the county jail. Almost 70
percent of those admitted are facing lesser charges (misdemeanors, violations, or infractions).
Half of all those detained are set free within two
days.

Rockland County uses its jails quite differ-
ently. For every 100 persons arrested in 1977, only
16 were detained in jail. Rockland's courts were
less likely than Rensselaer's to send persons not
charged with felonies to jail. Those few who were
detained were typically facing more serious charges
than in Rensselaer, and they stayed longer in jail
before making bail. As Table 5.5 shows, the median
detention period in Rockland was four days, in contrast to two in Rensselaer.

In Westchester the pattern was still different.
Forty-three out of every 100 persons arrested were
detained in jail; 54 percent of all admissions were
facing felony charges. Not only does Westchester
remand a comparatively high proportion of arrested
persons; it also keeps them the longest. The median stay was four days as in Rockland, but the half
that did not get out during those four days was detained longer than in the other two counties. That
is, the average detention period in Westchester
jails was thirteen days, in Rockland eleven, and
Rensselaer eight.

There were also big differences in the lengths
of sentences imposed by the county courts. Table
5.5 shows that in Rensselaer the median sentence was
almost six times longer than in Rockland, and in
Westchester almost seven times longer.

TABLE 5.5
Jail Use Patterns in Three Counties, 1977

	Rockland	Rensselaer	Westchester
Jail Admissions per 100 arrests[a]	16	49	43
Percentage of Admissions charged with felonies	62%	32%	54%
Median Detention (days)	4	2	4
Average Detention (days)	11	8	13
Median Sentence (days)	8	46	55
Capacity (persons)	99	110	260
Average Daily Census, 1977	69	48	228
Highest Daily Census, 1977	96	70	265

Source: Sheriffs' Reports, New York State Commission of Correction, 1977

[a]Estimated from New York State Division of Criminal Justice Services figures.

Controlling Jail Costs by Reducing
Prisoner Populations

Some of the high costs of jailing could be reduced
by better management. An even more effective cost-
control strategy would be to make significant reductions in the use of these institutions. Criminal
justice professionals generally agree that present
reliance on jails is excessive and -- by extension -- that we needlessly pay the cost of locking
up persons who do not seriously threaten public
safety.[19] Most persons who are detained in jail after arrest either have their cases dismissed, only
to return to the community, or are convicted of
charges that are not serious enough to require incarceration. Statewide data are not available but
the New York City information supports this asser-
tion. In 1977, 36 percent of all cases arraigned
in New York City courts were dismissed prior to
trial. Of those convicted, 68 percent received sentences which did not require imprisonment. Twenty-
eight percent were given local jail sentences, but
half were out within thirty days. Only 10 percent
were sent to state prison. [20] Despite the low proportion of persons ultimately deemed dangerous
enough to require a prison or long jail sentence,
most of those arrested had to spend some time in a
local jail before adjudication of their cases.

Sending fewer of these people to jail and
thereby reducing the prisoner population requires a
coordinated effort on the part of many different local agencies. No single agency exercises effective
control over jails and how they are used. As recog-
nized by the National Advisory Commission on Criminal Justice Standards and Goals:

> By tradition, the detention of unconvicted
> persons has fallen outside the jurisdiction
> of corrections, the courts, and police.
> Judges seldom order persons detained pending
> trial; they simply set bail. Prosecutors
> and defenders do not lock people up; they
> merely argue their recommendations to the
> court. Sheriffs and wardens make no deten-
> tion decisions; they only act as custodians
> for those who fail to gain pretrial release.
> Taken together, these abdications relegate
> the pretrial process to the role of step-
> child in the criminal justice system and
> explain why the problem remains so trouble-
> some. [21]

This fragmentation of responsibility means that jailing policies are the outcome of a complex web of individual agency interests. Police often make the first decision to place somebody in custody by placing them under physical arrest. Other options exist which would avert the high cost of jailing. For example, persons could be issued a summons for minor offenses rather than being put in jail; this is a common practice with traffic violations.

Judges regulate the number of detention prisoners in jail by a bail decision made at the time of arraignment. Some persons charged with felonies are held until trial without bail, but most are required to post bail or are released after promising to return to court when scheduled. In some New York counties bail agencies evaluate the likelihood of a defendant's returning for trial by verifying the defendant's ties to the community. (In eighteen counties this is done by probation departments; in some others by private or quasi-public agencies such as New York City's Criminal Justice Agency.) Some counties also have pretrial diversion agencies which provide a variety of social services to defendants released to their custody. Judges sometimes use these services to justify release without bail (a practice called ROR or "release on recognizance"). Unfortunately, these services exist in only a minority of counties.

The cost of jailing is also affected by the speed of the courts, the prosecutors, and the defense counsels in disposing of cases where the defendant is awaiting trial in jail. Once convicted, the length of time the offender waits in custody before sentencing depends in large measure on how quickly the probation department completes its presentencing investigation for the courts.

Coordinated policy making is further complicated by the fact that each of the agencies is responsible to different governing bodies. Police, for example, are generally municipal employees. District attorneys, public defenders, and probation departments are county employees. Parole boards are agents of the state government, and the courts will be fully incorporated by the state in the near future.

Even though the responsibility for jail use is fragmented among a number of agencies, efforts to reduce the numbers of people in jails have in fact been successful. However, these are generally undertaken only in response to severe overcrowding or riots. New York City, for example, sharply reduced

the number of pretrial detainees in its city jails
following a wave of jail riots in 1970. Westchester
and Rockland county officials also take steps to reduce their jail inmate populations when overcrowding
occurs.

When the pretrial prisoner population presses
against capacity in Westchester, the commissioner
of corrections notifies the county executive, the
chief judge, and the New York State Commission of
Correction. Courts speed up dispositions, lower
bails, and the probation department quickens the
processing of presentence investigations. During
1976, for example, it took an average of eight
weeks to complete a presentence investigation and
report. Under pressure from the courts and the
jail administrators, the time spent on this task
was cut in half during 1977, which allowed the
courts to significantly reduce detention time
between conviction and sentencing.[22]

The warden of the Rockland County jail has
established a more routine reporting practice.
Every Friday he tells the judges how many vacant
beds remain and he even identifies persons he
thinks could be released on recognizance. He has
personally taken some individuals back to the
courts and recommended release.[23]

Controlling Costs by Improving
Bail Decision Making

The practice of manipulating bail and pretrial release decisions to alleviate jail overcrowding is a
practice not condoned by law. According to the
statutes, the decision should be based instead on
the probability that the defendant will appear in
court when required. The courts are also required
to consider the nature of the offenses for which
the person was arrested, the defendant's past criminal history, employment and financial resources,
the weight of the evidence against him or her, the
penalty which could be imposed upon conviction, and
the defendant's "character, reputation, habits and
mental condition."[24] There is no legal basis for
considering such factors as jail conditions, cost
of imprisonment, or overcrowding.

In spite of this, we have seen that bail decisions in some jurisdictions are indeed affected by
the availability of cell space. When the courts
release a larger proportion of persons either on
their own recognizance or by lowering bail significantly, are they endangering public safety?

Information is not available which would directly answer this question, but there is good reason to conclude that the public safety is not more
seriously imperiled by a policy of releasing
greater numbers of persons. More importantly, it
is probable that more defendants could be released
on a continuing basis (and not simply during times
of crisis) without a substantially greater threat
to public safety. This is because judges in many
jurisdictions are undoubtedly locking up many people who would not commit another crime if released
and would show up in court when required.

The bail release decision is a form of gam-
bling, and judges are quite reasonably conservative
in placing their bets. One can never know with
certainty if a given defendant will not appear in
court if released. Our current knowledge of human
behavior does not allow us to make risk-free predictions like this. Like it or not, judges are
saddled with the necessity of having to make in-
herently risky decisions. They are required to
balance what they see as the risk to the community
with considerations of fairness (and, perhaps,with
other factors such as the availability of cell
space).

Given this circumstance, it is predictable
that many judges tend to be overcautious, hedging
their bets by setting higher bails than would be
necessary to insure the defendants' future appearance in court. It is likely that many of these
defendants who cannot make bail would appear in
court if released. The implication of this is that
some defendants are being unnecessarily detained at
a high cost to the taxpayers.

One strategy for reducing the pretrial detention population and costs is to assist the courts
in their ability to make more accurate assessments
of risk. Although predictors of future criminality
remain poorly developed, a technique has been re-
fined which quite accurately predicts whether a defendant is likely to return to court when required.
In New York City, for example, the Criminal Justice
Agency interviews all defendants prior to arraignment and evaluates their character, occupational
and residential stability, and the strength of
their family ties. For each defendant a score is
calculated which indicates the likelihood of compliance with orders to appear in court. On the basis of a given score, the agency then either recommends that the courts release the defendant on recognizance, makes a qualified recommendation, or no

recommendation at all.

Studies consistently show the strength of community ties to be accurate predictors of likeliness to appear. For example, in the last quarter of 1977 only 2.5 percent of all those recommended by the Criminal Justice Agency and released by the courts willfully failed to appear at a future court appointment. Of those not recommended by the agency but released by the courts nonetheless, the rate of willfull failure to appear was four times as high (10.1 percent).[25]

Providing arraignment judges with this kind of information has been shown to be a cost-effective method of reducing spending for local jails.[26] Organizations providing this service exist in only a third of New York State's counties. Creating similar services in the other counties would appear to be a sensible strategy for reducing local corrections costs.

Reducing Jail Costs by Creating
Alternative Forms of Supervision

Detaining persons in jails is an extremely expensive way to make sure they appear for adjudication. For those who cannot make bail and lack strong community ties, other nonmonetary forms of control might effectively ensure the defendant's future court appearances. These include such programs as releasing the defendant to a third party, either individuals or organizations.

The defendant could be required to check in with these organizations at specified intervals. If judges released defendants who would not have been otherwise released to these organizations, a significant financial gain would be realized. Not only would the high cost of incarceration be avoided, but jobs and schooling would not be disrupted, and families would continue to be supported.

Saving Money by Changing
Arrest Procedures

Still another alternative is for the police to refrain from jailing the defendant in the first place. New York City police began in 1964 to issue court summonses called desk appearance tickets to persons charged with less than felony offenses. This procedure avoids the injustice of locking up people who are almost certainly not going to receive sentences of imprisonment if convicted.[27] It also

avoids the high cost of jailing, and it saves police the time and money spent to process the defendant through booking and arraignment. The Police
Department estimates that approximately five hours
of police time is saved each time a summons is used
instead of a physical arrest. [28] This is five hours
which patrolmen can spend on the streets rather
than in the stationhouses and the courts.

Finally, savings in jail costs could also be
generated by sentencing more convicted persons not
to jail but to the payment of fines, or restitution
to the victim, or to the performance of some form
of public service. These alternative sanctions
have profitably been used in several European countries as well as in some American jurisdictions. [29]
Because these and other sentencing alternatives offer opportunities for reducing state prison costs
as well as local corrections costs, they are more
fully discussed in the conclusion to this report.

SUMMARY

During calendar year 1977 approximately $240 mil-
lion was spent to operate county jails and penitentiaries outside New York City. The cost of jailing
a single inmate that year ranged from an estimated
$14,065 to $24,855 annually, or $38.50 to $68 per
day, depending upon the county.

These statewide figures are only approxima-
tions, however, for the reporting systems do not
allow a precise determination of jail costs. Jails
in all counties except for Westchester and New York
City's five counties are run by their sheriffs, and
some accounts mix correction costs with other unre-
lated expenses such as spending for highway patrol.
The accounts also omit some jail-related costs which
are borne by other government agencies and accounts.

For a more exact analysis of local spending
for corrections, expenditures were examined in
three counties and New York City. (New York City
jail costs are analysed separately in Chapter 6 because of their magnitude and complexity.) The average costs of jailing a single prisoner in these
three counties ranged from $16,400 to $29,700 per
year, or $45 to $81 per day. In Westchester County
alone, the cost ranged from $20,600 to $29,700 per

year, depending upon which building the prisoners were locked in.

The variation in cost is due primarily to differences in the costs of staffing and medical care. Salary levels vary dramatically from one county to another. Medical costs in the three sampled counties ranged from $3.25 per prisoner day in one county to $12.87 in another.

Control over the cost of jails is fragmented because the decisions made by many different actors and agencies have an impact on jail admission rates and length of stay. Costs are affected, for example, by police arrest policies, court bail policies, and the speed of probation departments in completing presentence investigations. Despite this fragmentation, officials in two of the three counties sampled indicated that a coordinated reduction in jail population is made when overcrowding becomes severe. This shows that a more sustained effort could be made not only to relieve overcrowding but also to lower the pretrial detention population in the jails over the long term, thereby easing the fiscal drain on local taxpayers. The wide variation in both pretrial detention and jail sentencing practices among the three counties studied suggests that there is room for lowering costs by more frugal use of pretrial detention, by changing arrest and bail release practices, and by expanding alternatives to imprisonment for convicted persons. Most prisoners do not need the maximum-security supervision of local jail.

Not only are there differences in how counties use their jails, but there is also wide variation in the quality and level of services from one county to another. This is partly because local jails, unlike the state prisons, depend upon local taxes for their operation. Counties with larger tax bases are able to afford better jails; many of the less wealthy counties are saddled with antiquated and sub-standard facilities. A obvious strategy for upgrading local corrections would be to establish a program of state aid to local corrections. Several such arrangements have been developed in other states and deserve examination for their possible use in New York State.

6
Jails in New York City

The Department of Correction in New York City is the largest municipal system in the United States. During 1978 it operated eight primary institutions with a capacity of 7,500 prisoners.[1] At the heart of department operations is Rikers Island, a 400-acre complex located in the East River with perhaps the largest concentration of prisoners in the Western world. During the year ended June 30, 1978 the New York City jail system cost the taxpayers an estimated $171.2 million to operate, at an average of $24,855 per prisoner per year, or $68 per day.[2]

Department operations are far more complex than those of any other local jail system in the state because it serves not one jurisdiction but rather five different counties. Elsewhere in the state jails have a simpler one-to-one relationship with courts, prosecutors, legal defense, and probation agencies. The network with which the department must deal is five times more extensive.

This chapter

- describes the complex character of this municipal jail system;
- reveals the cost of jailing in New York City;
- estimates the widely differing costs of each institution operated by the Department of Correction;
- illustrates how the courts regulate the use of jails and--by extension--their costs; and finally,
- describes plans for building new jails in New York City.

The Multitude of Jails in New York City

Outside New York City newly arrested persons are
generally held in local lock-ups and are then transferred to county jails after being arraigned before
a judge. In New York City the Department of Correction not only operates these court detention pens
but also jails for detained prisoners awaiting
trial, jails for sentenced prisoners, and a number
of medical facilities.

On Rikers Island six housing facilities and
twenty-three support-service buildings contain over
3.2 million square feet of floor space.[3] These include the New York City House of Detention for Men
(HDM); the Correctional Institution for Men (CIFM),
which houses sentenced men; the Correctional Institution for Women (CIFW), housing both detained and
sentenced women; the Adolescent Reception and Detention Center (ARDC) for detained male teenagers;
the Mental Health Center; and the Rikers Island
Hospital.*

Off the island are the detention jails in three
boroughs: the Queens, Bronx and Brooklyn houses of
detention. Sentenced work-release prisoners are
placed in the Brooklyn and Manhattan residential
facilities.**

The numbers of people processed by this system
are staggering. Over 250,000 persons were held in
custody prior to a first court appearance during
1977. Of these, 55,000 were returned to the department after arraignment for detention. Over 18,000
sentenced inmates were admitted to the department
during the same year.[4] As in all local jail systems,
the turnover of prisoners is very high. Nonetheless, the average daily number of persons under custody during fiscal 1978 was 6,887 persons (*or 96 percent of capacity*), 64 percent of whom were in detention awaiting trial.[5] To operate this huge system
the department employed in fiscal 1978 over 4,000
persons, or about three employees for every five
prisoners in custody. [6]

All housing institutions, but especially the
detention facilities, receive and discharge prison-

---

*An additional building, the Anna M. Kross Center,
was not in regular use during fiscal 1978.
**The Brooklyn residential facility was closed on
June 30, 1978.

ers to a citywide collection of court detention
pens operated by the department. These are found
in each borough's Family, Traffic, Criminal and
Supreme Courts, and Manhattan's Narcotics Court.
The department is responsible for custodial super-
visition of prisoners during court proceedings, for
persons committed directly from court, for newly arrested individuals awaiting Criminal Court arraignment, and for prisoners in court meeting with prosecution, defense, and probation personnel.

The medical needs of inmates required that the
department not only operate two facilities on Rikers
Island (Rikers Island Hospital and Mental Health
Center), but also provide security and transportation to and from prison wards in three municipal
hospitals: Bellevue, Kings County, and Elmhurst
General. During 1977 these five medical facilities
housed over 500 prisoners per day. [7]

The Cost of Corrections in New York City

During fiscal 1978 taxpayers spent $171.177 million
to operate the New York City jails. The cost of
keeping a single prisoner for a year averaged
$24,855, or $68 per day.

Table 6.1 distinguishes the various costs which
make up this $171 million. Two different "layers"
of expenditures can be distinguished: those made
directly by the Department of Correction, and those
by other agencies in support of the jail system.

First layer costs include salaries, salary adjustments,* some fringe benefits,** and other-than-

---

*These include vacation relief, terminal leave,
longevity pay, and overtime.
**The department's share of fringe benefits includes
cost of living adjustments, shift and assignment
differentials, holiday pay, welfare and annuity contributions, and uniform allowances. These amount to
20.4% of total uniformed force salaries and 15% of
civilian salaries. CETA workers earn only cost of
living adjustments. [8] (Uniformed workers also receive free meals while on duty, which represents an
additional benefit of about 3% of salary. [9] This has
not been separated out from the cost of food in the

TABLE 6.1
Expenditures for New York City Corrections by Object,
FY 1978

Paid by
Department of Correction

Salaries	$ 68,175,301	(40%)
Salary Adjustments	10,168,126	(6%)
Other Than Personal Services	18,510,000	(11%)
Fringe Benefits	13,230,265	(7.7%)

Paid by
Other Agency Accounts

Fringe Benefits	8,345,000	(4.9%)
Retirement Fund Contributions	27,527,895	(16%)
Outside Services (Medical, Education, Work Release)	25,221,000	(15%)
	$171,177,587	(100%)

Sources:

Salaries, Adjustments: Department of Correction, Payroll Division (includes expenditures and encumbrances)
Other Than Personal Services (OTPS): Department of Correction, Fiscal Control (total fiscal year 1978, as of 9/10/78)
Retirement Fund Contribution Rates: New York City Office of Management and Budget
Fringe Benefit Rates: New York City Office of Management and Budget, and New York City Department of Correction
Outside Services: *Medical* -- computed from information in New York City Department of Health, Prison Health Services, letter of July 24, 1978, and New York City Health and Hospitals Corporation, letter of July 31, 1978. *Education* -- computed from estimated fiscal year 1976 costs in Coopers & Lybrand, "The Cost of Incarceration in New York City," National Council on Crime and Delinquency (N.J., 1978). *Work release/community residential facilities* -- expenditure data supplied by Richard Aneiro, Model Cities, New York City Mayor's Office; estimated fringe and pension costs added.

personal-services, all charged to the department expense budget. These direct costs are the most visible and are often the only ones used in reporting the cost of corrections. But these are only a portion of the total; in fiscal 1978 these direct costs amounted to $110.1 million, only 64 percent of the total costs of jailing in the city.

The second and less visible layer is made up of those costs not directly charged to the department budget but nonetheless attributable to jailing operations. They include additional fringe benefits* and retirement contributions which are charged not to the department but rather to the New York City "Miscellaneous" budget. These retirement fund conributions amounted to approximately $27.528 million during fiscal 1978, or about 16 percent of total corrections costs. Uniformed personnel were more handsomely rewarded than civilians. Retirement fund payments for the former amounted to 42.5 percent of every dollar paid in gross salary; contributions for civilians were at the rate of 32 percent on the salary dollar.[10]

(The combined fringe benefits and retirement fund contributions paid out by both the department and the New York City "Miscellaneous" budget amounted to *72 percent* of salaries during fiscal 1978. Uniformed employees earned at a rate of 75.1 percent, civilians at 60.7 percent of salary.)

Also in the layer of secondary costs are expenditures charged to other New York City agencies for services provided to the Department of Correction. These were substantial in fiscal 1978: we were able to identify at least $25.2 million, or 15 percent of total corrections costs. These included medical and mental health services provided to prisoners by the Health and Hospitals Corporation, the Prison Health Service of the Department of Health, and by Montefiore Hospital. These cost $22,582,000 in fiscal 1978. Also identified were the costs for educational programs provided by the New York City boards of education and higher education; these cost $1,889,000. Yet another expenditure was $750,000 for community residential facilities, funded through the Model Cities program in the Mayor's Office.

---

following pages, and has therefore not been calculated into the fringe payment here.)
*These include payments for social security, health insurance, supplemental welfare, unemployment insurance, and workman's compensation.

There were other additional indirect costs
which were incurred by the operation of the jails
but could not be estimated. These included general
governmental overhead, costs incurred by private organizations providing direct services to inmates,
and medical costs absorbed by city agencies because
complete reimbursement was not made. Nor were we
able to allocate the department's share of city debt
service payments since both short-term borrowing and
long-term financing are included in the fiscal 1978
retirement of debt. (Outstanding debt on department
capital construction was $69.191 million at the end
of fiscal year 1978.[11])

What the Corrections Dollar Buys

What the taxpayers bought with their $24,855 expend-
iture for one prisoner-year during fiscal 1978 is
perhaps best shown by a disclosure of how corrections monies were spent. Unfortunately, the accounting systems in use do not classify expenditures
in a manner which adequately describes the various
services purchased with tax dollars. To portray accurately the relative importance of these different
services, the available fiscal information was reclassified to produce Table 6.2. Note that Table
6.2 not only shows the costs of each activity in
New York City jails but also compares them with the
way monies are spent in the state prison system.
Furthermore, the functional costs which make up the
average annual per prisoner expenditure of $24,855
in New York City are shown.
    The basic tool for this reclassification was a
1978 survey done by the Department of Correction examining all work assignments, both civilian and uniformed, throughout the agency. (Community residential facilities and central administrative units
were not surveyed, however.) The survey did not
simply identify job titles but rather recorded the
precise character of work actually performed at each
assigned post for each 15-minute period. This survey enables us to estimate how expenditures were
distributed across the seven broad types of activities.[12]

TABLE 6.2
Comparing the Costs of Different Activities
in New York City Jails and New York State Prisons, FY 1978

	NYC Jails			NYS Prisons
	Total Annual Cost	Annual Cost per Prisoner		
Security	$ 61,526,623	$ 8,923	(35.9%)	(50%)
Administration	24,010,912	3,480	(14%)	(10.5%)
Plant Operations and Transportation/ Prisoner Processing	17,283,936	2,510	(10.1%)	(11.7%)
Prisoner Necessities	45,867,412	6,661	(26.8%)	(15%)
Programs	7,523,204	1,094	(4.4%)	(10%)
Industries	2,499,439	373	(1.5%)	(2%)
Other	12,467,061	1,814	(7.3%)	(0.3%)
	$171,177,587	$24,855	(100%)	(100%)

Sources: Computed from information provided by New York City
Department of Correction, Office of Management and Budget,
Department of Health, Health and Hospitals Corporation, May-
or's Office (Model Cities program), National Council on Crime
and Delinquency (Coopers & Lybrand). State prison figures
computed from information in New York State Department of
Correctional Services tables and letter dated July 19, 1978.

Security

As in the state prison system, the largest expenditure was for security. The Department of Correction
distinguishes among three different functions of the
uniformed staff: security and movement control,
housing, and receiving room. Each of these parallels
the activities by the uniformed officers in the
state prisons, so we have combined them into a single category here. Table 6.3 shows the cost of each
function.
    Security and movement control duties include
patrol, searching for contraband, escorting inmates
from one part of the department's sytem to another,

TABLE 6.3
Cost of Security and Custody in
New York City Jails, FY 1978

Security and Movement Control	$28,289,344
Housing	27,689,799
Receiving Room	5,547,480
	$61,526,623

Sources: Computed from information provided by New York City
Department of Correction and Office of Management and Budget.

and the general control of all prisoner movement.

Housing duties include counting prisoners during the course of the day to make sure all are accounted for, keeping records of prisoner movements to and from housing areas, and supervising all prisoner services in the cellblocks or dormitories.

Receiving room duties involve the admission and discharge of prisoners. Officers assigned here search prisoners, determine their identities from fingerprints and photographs, collect personal property, verify legal documents, issue personal hygiene articles, arrange for transport, and provide security during the intake medical examinations.

Administration, Plant Operations,
Transportation

During fiscal 1978 nearly $41 million was spent for administration, plant operations, and transportation in the city jail system (Table 6.4).

Proportionately more was spent on these activities in the New York City system than in the state prison system. Whereas administrative costs consumed 10.5 percent of total state prison expenditures, they amounted to 14 percent in the city. The city system spends more (in both relative and absolute terms) than the state for transportation. The city facilities housing detention prisoners incur the heaviest transportation costs -- a not unexpected finding since detained prisoners have to be carried back and forth to court. During fiscal 1978

TABLE 6.4
Overhead and Prisoner Processing Costs
in New York City Jails, FY 1978

Administration	$24,010,912
Plant Operations	
Maintenance	10,925,661
Sanitation	962,384
Transportation	5,395,891
	$41,294,848

Sources: Computed from information provided by New York City
Department of Correction and Office of Management and Budget.

there were 174,000 detention prisoner transfers to
court.[13] All totaled, the Department of Correction
made over 400,000 transfers of all kinds over a dis-
tance of more than 800,000 miles.[14]

Prisoner Necessities

During fiscal 1978, 27 percent of the expense of
jailing in New York City, or $45.9 million, was for
various prisoner necessities, including health services, food, prisoner wages, visiting, commissary, and
laundry. During the same fiscal year only 15 percent of state prison expenditures was for these
necessities (Table 6.5).

   Medical Care: The difference between state and
city expenditures for prisoner necessities is almost
entirely accounted for by the greater cost for medical services in New York City. Not only did the
city jails spend proportionately more of their total
expenditures on medical services than the state (15
percent versus 4 percent); they also spent more ab-
solutely: $25.8 million versus $10.1 million in the
state prisons. This reflects in part the different
medical needs of city prisoners. During fiscal 1978
8,732 of the admitted prisoners were narcotics addicts requiring detoxification and close medical attention.[15] Others suffered from gunshot wounds and
other injuries. A New York County jail screening
program found that 23 percent of the prisoners

TABLE 6.5
Cost of Prisoner Necessities in
New York City Jails, FY 1978

Medical Services	$25,833,152
Food	12,667,306
Prisoner Wages	1,365,000
Miscellaneous Other	
Visiting	3,220,908
Commissary	1,985,000
Laundry	796,046
	$45,867,412

Sources: Computed from information provided by New York City
Department of Correction, Office of Management and Budget,
Department of Health, and Health and Hospitals Corporation

required immediate medical attention.[16] By the time
the state prisons received these people, they were
generally weaned from their addictions and had
healed whatever wounds they might have had when
arrested.

The New York City Department of Correction, unlike the state prison system, is not a direct pro-
vider of medical services but contracts with outside
vendors.[17] Emergency medical, surgical, and psychiatric treatment is provided by three municipal hospitals (Bellevue, Kings County, and Elmhurst General) and the Rikers Island Hospital. The medical
staff in the municipal hospitals is under the jurisdiction of the New York City Health and Hospitals
Corporation. All other medical and mental health
care in facilities operated by the Department of
Correction is provided by the Prison Health Service,
a division of the New York City Department of
Health. In four institutions, however, Prison
Health Service does not directly provide medical
services but instead contracts them out to Montefiore Hospital. (Montefiore services the New York
City House of Detention for Men, the Adolescent
Reception and Detention Center, and the New York
City Correctional Institutions for Men and Women.)

Food: The department served over nine million meals to prisoners and employees during fiscal 1978, or about 25,000 every day.[18] These cost a total of $12.7 million of which $5.4 million went for the purchase of foodstuffs, and the remainder was spent on salaries and benefits for kitchen employees.[19]

The daily cost of the food in prisoners' meals was only $1.42.[20]

Twenty-three percent of the meals served were for department employees. Whereas civilians are charged $1.65 for their meals, uniformed employees receive them free of charge. These meals cost an estimated $2.61 apiece, and are therefore an additional fringe benefit (about 3 percent of salary).[21] If uniformed personnel were charged for these meals at the same rate as civilians, an additional $618,000 could be available for prisoners' food, about an 18 percent increase.

Prisoner Wages and Subsidies: Sentenced prisoners and some pretrial detainees are paid between 20¢ and 35¢ per hour for work. They are also give "gate money" and clothing upon release. The total amount of money given prisoners during fiscal 1978 amounted to approximately $1.4 million.

Miscellaneous Other Necessities: The department now allows "contact" visits for the majority of prisoners. (That is, prisoners are not separated from their visitors by a partition.) During fiscal 1978 there were 160,000 contact visits and another 61,000 restricted visits.[22] Because Rikers Island is difficult to get to from most parts of the city, prisoners only received an average of one visit every two weeks. Prisoners in the more accessible Bronx, Queens, and Brooklyn jails had twice as many. The cost of these visits to the department was almost $3.2 million in fiscal 1978. This represented almost 2 percent of the total cost of jailing during that year. (State prisons are much less accessible and prisoners there receive fewer visits. During fiscal 1978, 0.2 percent of the total cost of the prison system was for visiting facilities.)

The $796,046 spent for laundry was not for cleaning prisoners' personal clothing but rather for cleaning linen and uniforms. At present, prisoners must wash their own clothes in the cellblocks or dormitories. (This will be changed in the future pursuant to a recently issued standard by the Board of Correction, the "watchdog" agency of the city jail system.)

Programs

Whereas about 10 percent of state prison costs are
for programs, only 4.4 percent, or $7.5 million,
of city costs were for social, educational, religious, and recreational services. This is partly
because state prisons and local jails have different mandates; detained prisoners in jails have not
been sentenced to a term of "rehabilitation." (An
average of 64 percent of those under custody during
fiscal 1978 were pretrial detainees.[23])
    Educational programs are operated not only by
the Department of Correction but also by the New
York City boards of education and higher education;
(the cost of these latter services is estimated to
have been $1,889,000 in fiscal 1978).
    Other programs include the availability of le-
gal libraries to help prisoners prepare their court
cases, entertainment, physical recreation, arts and
crafts, religious services, and counseling.

Industries

Department industries manufacture a small number of
articles, such as blankets and mattresses, all for
use within the city jails. (This differs from the
state prison industries which manufacture goods used
by a wide variety of government agencies.) During
fiscal 1978, $2.5 million was spent on these indus-
tries, or about 1.5 percent of the total expenditure
for New York City jails.

Other

These are expenditures of $8.8 million (5.2 percent
of the total cost of jailing) which are not readily
assignable to other categories. They include emergency relief and transfers. The cost of one facility not in use during 1978 -- the Anna M. Kross Center -- is included here because no functional break-
down of services in this unit was available. Furthermore, this includes 16 percent of the other-
than-personal-service costs, as well as 3 percent
of the $25.2 million spent by outside agencies in
support of corrections. These latter could not be
distributed to each of the various functions.

Distinguishing the Cost of Housing
Sentenced and Detention Prisoners

The daily per prisoner cost of $68 is an *average* for
men and women, sentenced prisoners as well as persons detained while awaiting trial. Because certain
criminal justice reforms can affect sentenced prisoners but not detainees (or vice versa), an adequate
cost analysis of these reforms requires separating
the cost of jailing each of these two types of prisoners. For example, a change in bail policy directly affects persons awaiting trial.* To estimate
accurately the savings or increased costs produced
when judges lower bails or simply release more defendants on their own recognizance, one must know
the cost of detention and not simply the average
cost for all prisoners.**
     Because the New York City Department of Correc-
tion has specialized units to house each different
type of prisoner, the logical solution is to determine the amount it costs to operate each separate
unit. Unfortunately, this cannot be done except
for almost all of the personal service costs.[24]
Adequate information is not available to distribute
the other-than-personal-service costs or the $25.221
million incurred by outside agencies. Additionally,
personal service expenditures for central administration could not be distributed to each separate
facility. In sum: Table 6.6 summarizes the distribution of personal service costs for each institution. These constituted almost 70 percent, on the
average, of the total cost of imprisonment during
fiscal 1978.
     The differences in these payroll costs are dra-
matic, and they obviously reflect the way each facility is staffed.[25] The jail for sentenced men

_____

*Bail policies also affect the size of the sentenced
population because those in detention at time of
trial are significantly more likely to be sentenced
to terms of incarceration than those at liberty.
See *Crimes, Criminals, and Courthouses: Sentencing Reform in
Three New York Counties,* a forthcoming publication of
the Citizens' Inquiry on Parole and Criminal Justice, Inc.
**The marginal costs of reducing jail populations
must also be determined -- an exercise far more
complex than can be undertaken here.

(New York City Correctional Institution for Men)
spends the least money on personal services and has
the greatest number of prisoners per guard (5 to 1).
(In Table 6.6 the cost of this facility is used as
the baseline against which all other costs are compared in column 3.) Detention facilities are relatively more expensive to staff: the most expensive
is the New York City Adolescent Reception and Detention Center which has 2.7 prisoners per guard
and costs 87 percent more to staff than the jail for
sentenced adult men. The jail for both sentenced
and detained women has a very low prisoner-to-guard
ratio (1.7:1) and the cost of staffing is at least
$29,740 per prisoner, or about 1.5 times the cost
of NYCCIFM.

Hospital wards are the most expensive. The
extraordinarily high cost of correctional personnel
in these facilities does not even include the costs
of medical staffs in the Health and Hospitals Corporation or the Department of Health Prison Health
Service.

Even though the total operating cost of each
facility cannot be determined, it is clear that reduction in jail population, especially the detention
population, would produce considerable savings.

Reducing the Use of Jails:
The New York City Example

The regulation of jail populations -- and by extension, jail costs -- is exercised by the police,
prosecutors, and the courts. A comparison of jail
use patterns in Chapter 5 shows a good deal of variety from one county to another. A brief examination
of the historical trends in New York City provides a
suggestive illustration of how jail populations are
affected by changes in court policy.

Despite an enormous increase in the numbers of
arrests in New York City between 1967 and 1977, the
number of persons put in jail to await trial decreased precipitously. Figure 6.1 shows that the
volume of arrest cases placed in the court detention
pens for arraignment increased from about 140,000 in
1967 to about 264,000 in 1977. During the same period, the percentage of those persons sent (remand-
ed) to jail after being charged in court declined

TABLE 6.6
Cost of Staff on New York City Department of Correction Payroll, by Institution, FY 1978

	Total Personal Service Cost	The Cost of Personal Service per Inmate-year	Percentage over least expensive institution on inmate-day basis	# of inmates per correction officer
	(millions)			
Detention				
Brooklyn House of Detention for Men	$12.7	$17,280	49%	3.4
Bronx House of Detention for Men	9.2	18,310	57	3.1
NYC House of Detention for Men	25.0	15,920	37	4.4
NYC Adolescent Reception and Detention Center	18.8	21,700	87	2.7
Queens House of Detention for Men	7.9	16,390	41	4.2
Sentence				
NYC Correctional Institution for Men	20.6	11,630	Baseline	5.1
NYC Correctional Institution for Women	10.1	29,740	156	1.7
Hospital				
Bellevue	3.2	42,850	268	1.0
Elmhurst General	0.9	55,020	373	.8
Kings County	2.9	46,970	304	.9
Rikers Island	3.4	23,430	101	2.2
Mental Health Center	4.7	16,720	44	3.4

Sources: *Institutional Personal Services:* NYC Department of Correction, Payroll Division. *Estimated fringe and pension:* NYC Office of Management and Budget, NYC Department of Correction. *Allocated Personal Services:* See note 24. *Inmate-Officer Ratios:* NYC Department of Correction, Payroll Division, Records and Statistics.

124

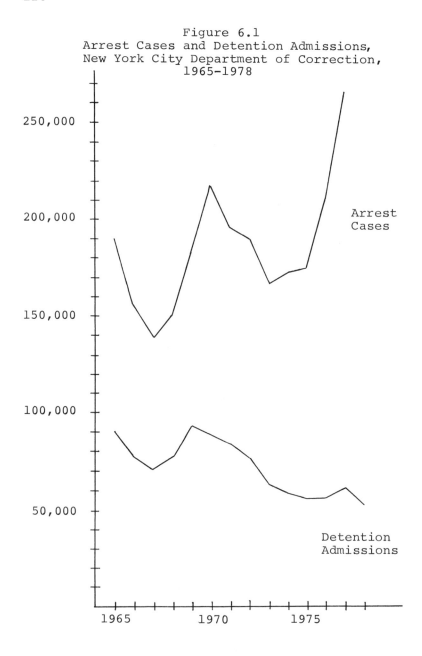

Figure 6.1
Arrest Cases and Detention Admissions,
New York City Department of Correction,
1965-1978

Sources: New York City Department of Correction,
Annual Statistical Reports, 1965-1978

from about 48 to 20 percent in 1977. The consequence of this was a sharp decline in the number of
detention admissions, as Figure 6.1 illustrates.
This decline has been paralleled by a reduction in
the size of the detention population. Between 1969
and 1977 the average number of persons in pretrial
detention has decreased by about 3,000 persons.* [26]
The decline in jail admissions was caused by a number of factors, but three seem to have been predomi-
nant: the development of the Release on Recognizance (ROR) program, the response of the court to
overcrowding in the jails, and the "front loading"
of the courts and prosecution, which employed greater numbers of experienced judges and prosecutors in
the earlier stages of criminal processing.

In the early 1960s the Vera Institute of Justice developed a program to encourage judges to release more persons awaiting trial without having to
post bail. A service was established which provided
judges with information regarding the probable risk
of releasing a defendant on his or her honor. As
indigent defendants awaited arraignment in Criminal
Court, they were questioned about their ties to the
community (residence, family ties, and employment);
these claims were then immediately verified in personal or telephone interviews. This verified information was then provided to the judge. If the defendant's community ties indicated a strong likelihood of returning to court when required, this pretrial service agency recommended release on the defendant's own recognizance without posting bail.
Evaluation of the service indicated that the extent
and duration of community ties was a good predictor
of risk, and the program was then given to the Department of Probation in 1964. [28]

Until 1968 the rate of remanding defendants to

---

*The reduction of the jail population produced by
declining admissions has been offset somewhat by a
longer pretrial custody period for those not released. This is partly because the detention population is increasingly composed of persons facing
high charges which take longer to dispose of in the
Supreme Court as well as persons who are held on no
bail. One survey found that in January 1978, 64% of
those in the House of Detention for Men were facing
A or B felony charges, the two highest levels. A
second survey a month later found that 48% of all
detainees in the custody of the department were held
without bail. [27]

jail after arraignment remained fairly stable, which
indicates that the bail-evaluation services were not
having a significant impact on the jail population.
It was not until other forces came into play that a
dramatic reduction in the pretrial detention population was achieved. By the 1960s the jails held the
largest number of prisoners in the city's history.*
In August 1970 there was a takeover by prisoners of
the Manhattan House of Detention (called "The
Tombs"), and a wave of rioting spread through the
other city jails. The courts responded by remanding
fewer arrested persons to jails, and it is not unlikely that judges began to rely more heavily upon
the risk predictions made by the Department of Probation pretrial service. Between July and September
1970, the remand rate decreased by 25 percent. The
longer-term result was a 13 percent decline in the
average detention population in the following year.[29]

Shortly after a new administrative judge for
New York City courts (Judge David Ross) was appointed in January 1971, a number of court reorganiza-
tions began to take place. More resources were put
into the earliest stages of the court processing
system to quicken the handling of cases -- a strategy called "front loading." Disposition-oriented
judges were assigned to the arraignment benches and
were encouraged to dispose of as many cases as possible rather than push them into more drawn-out
prosecutions. Night arraignment courts were established in the Bronx and Queens in 1971, and then
later in other boroughs. No data exist on the disposition rates at arraignment for that period, but a
comparison of the number of pending cases in the
courts at the end of 1970 and 1972 (59,400 and
16,900 respectively) indicates that the front-loading strategy did have a dramatic effect on quickening the resolution of cases brought before the
courts. [30]

Prosecution also began to front load its operation. In 1975 Early Case Assessment Bureaus were

---

*Total population (both sentenced and detained pris-
oners) was highest during the 1969-1972 period, with
a peak average census of almost 14,000 in 1970. The
sentenced prisoner population reached its high point
in 1971 and dropped off sharply after that. The average detention population reached its peak in 1969,
changed little in the following year, dropped off in
1971, and then increased again in 1972. Since then
it has declined steadily.

created in the Manhattan, Brooklyn, and Bronx District Attorneys' offices. Experienced prosecutors were put into the Complaint Rooms, where arraignment charges are drawn up, and they were encouraged to screen out weak cases from those which could be sent without delay to the grand jury for indictment on felonies without the intermediate processing in the lower Criminal Courts. One result was that more felony charges were reduced to misdemeanors at arraignment and disposed of. (In Brooklyn, for example, the percentage of felony arrest cases disposed of at arraignment increased from 13 to 26 percent after the bureau was established.[31]) Cases remaining in the courts were also processed faster. One evaluation of this innovation estimated that this front-loading strategy saved an estimated $2.25 million in pretrial detention costs from Brooklyn and Bronx cases alone.[32]

The combined effect of these and other factors produced a significant decline in the rate of remanding persons to jail to await trial. The average length of pretrial detention also declined.* This in turn reduced the size of the pretrial detention population by approximately 3,000 persons between 1969 and 1977. These court and prosecution reforms have generated substantial savings in the cost of jailing in New York City.

The Future of the New York City Jail System

City and state officials have begun planning the construction of an entirely new jail system in New York City to be completed by the mid-1980s. As discussed in Chapter 2, the Rikers Island complex would be leased by the state for sentenced prisoners. The scenario envisions the transfer of part of Rikers Island immediately, and then the construction of

---

*The average length of pretrial detention rose from eighteen days in 1965 to thirty-nine days in 1973, and then declined to twenty-six days in 1976. In 1977 the figures took an upturn; the average detention time during that year was thirty-two days. Preliminary 1979 figures show a continued lengthening of detention time. [33]

seven or eight replacement jails in four boroughs
(excluding Staten Island).[34] These are expected to
be 450- or 500-bed facilities which will be built
from the ground up at a construction cost of between $75,000 and $90,000 per bed. The evaluation
of possible sites is now underway. Once city prisoners are moved from Rikers to these new facilities,
the state would assume the vacant Rikers Island
cells.

The financing of this large-scale project will
come from the city's earnings on the lease of Rikers
Island to the state and from the city capital budget. The New York State legislature has set a $200
million ceiling on the payment to the city for this
lease, although additional funds will be required
for adequate renovation of Rikers Island. The present estimate of construction costs for the new city
jails is $360 million; the city is responsible for
all expenses over $200 million.

In addition to the construction of new jails,
existing jails will be renovated. The most advanced
of these plans is the proposed renovation of the
Manhattan House of Detention, otherwise known as
The Tombs. This jail, attached to the Criminal
Courts building in downtown Manhattan, was recon-
structed in 1940 for a capacity of 1,040 prisoners.
Notions about what constituted acceptable treatment
of jail prisoners changed in the ensuing years, and
finally, in 1974, a court decision in the case of
Rhem v. Malcolm directed that the jail be closed until
it met a number of minimum standards.[35]

In late 1978 city officials contracted with architects to devise a plan for the eighteen-month
renovation of The Tombs. The plan recommends rede-
signing the jail to accommodate approximately 400
prisoners (one cell per person except in the psychiatric ward) at a total construction cost of $35 mil-
lion. This renovation will cost over $75,000 per
bed.[36]

The total capacity of the new city system has
not yet been determined. Some officials prefer to
maintain the Department of Correction capacity at
the current level and this is the present plan.
Others believe that future city prison populations
will be reduced, given the demographic trends, the
possible extension of jail diversion programs, and a
more efficient arrest and bail process. Given the
high cost of constructing or even renovating jails,
as well as the large operating costs, the possibil-
ities of reducing the size of the jail system must
be assessed very closely. Overbuilding would be a
costly error.

SUMMARY

The largest local corrections system in the state
(and the largest municipal system in the country)
is the New York City network of jails, court pens,
and prison health services. During fiscal 1978 taxpayers spent $171.2 million to operate this correc-
tion system. The average cost of keeping one prisoner behind bars during that period was $24,855 per
year, or $68 per day.

The cost per prisoner varied widely among the
twelve different facilities which separate detention
from sentenced prisoners, men from women and adoles-
cents, and the healthy from the ill. The expenditure information available does not allow us to establish the total cost of each institution, but the
relative costs were estimated. The institution for
sentenced men was the least expensive to operate;
the facility for sentenced and detained women was
approximately 160 percent more expensive. In general, detention facilities were more expensive to operate than facilities for sentenced prisoners, and
the hospital wards even more expensive. Differences in the cost of each facility reflect differences in staffing levels.

The costs of various services throughout the
New York City jail system were estimated using a
survey of work assignments within the Department of
Crrection. For each prisoner during fiscal 1978 the
department spent, on average, $8,923 for security,
$3,480 for administration, $2,510 for transportation
and prisoner processing costs, $6,661 for various
prisoner necessities, $373 for the prison indus-
tries, and only $1,094 for education, religious, so-
cial, and recreational programs.

New York City is currently designing a new jail
system which will involve construction of seven new
jails in four of the five boroughs. This will cost
at least $400 million, $200 million of which is expected to be earned by leasing Rikers Island to the
state. The remainder will be paid out of New York
City capital funds. The capacity of this new jail
network has not yet been determined, although it is
not expected to exceed the current levels. Renova-

tion of "The Tombs," a Manhattan jail for detained prisoners, is planned at a cost of approximately $75,000 per bed. Construction costs of new jails could run as high as $90,000 per bed, exclusive of financing costs.

In the wake of the jail riots of 1970, a coordinated effort was undertaken to reduce the city prisoner population. By 1977 the average number of pretrial prisoners under custody had declined to about 4,500, or 3,000 below the 1969 levels. This reduction was achieved by devoting more resources to the earlier stages of prosecution and court processing, and by more frequent release of pretrial prisoners on their own recognizance. The history of this experience indicates that similar reforms in other jurisdictions could significantly lower the use of pretrial detention, which in turn would generate significant savings for taxpayers.

Conclusion

Criminal justice in New York State is a very costly
enterprise. During fiscal 1977-78 all levels of
government in the state spent approximately $2.8
billion of the taxpayers' dollars in the hope of
protecting the public.[1] This sum amounted to approximately 10 percent of all government spending
that year. Only public education and social services cost the taxpayer more.*

Most of this money went to police our communities, but over $600 million was spent on operating
what have been generously called "correctional"
agencies: prisons, jails, probation, and parole.
During 1977 alone they admitted more than 400,000
persons charged with or convicted of crimes.[3] The
number of people under some form of custody for
criminal charges is astoundingly high. On any given
day during 1977 about 90,000 adults, or one out of
every fifty-six male New Yorkers over the age of
fifteen, were confined in prison or jail, or were
under probation or parole supervision.[4]

Almost 90 percent of all admissions during 1977
were to the most expensive correctional agencies:
jails and prisons. The cost of this heavy reliance
on these institutions is enormous. For example, the
average cost of locking one person in a New York
City jail during 1977-78 was $68 per day, or $24,855
per year. During the same period, the average cost

---

*Social services include home relief, old age as-
sistance, medical assistance, aid to dependent
children, foster care, hospital care, burials, adult
care in private institutions, juvenile delinquent
care and payments to state-operated training
schools, assistance to the blind and disabled,
children's shelters, infirmaries, and public homes.[2]

131

for a year in the state prisons was $15,050 per
prisoner. The average length of stay in New York
City jails is thirty-eight days, and in state prison after conviction, twenty-seven months. Thus taxpayers spent approximately $36,000 to incarcerate a
single person in these penal facilities. This sum
does not include the costs of arrest, prosecution,
defense, and other courtroom costs.

Despite the large amounts involved in maintain-
ing our present correctional agencies, the specific
dollar costs are difficult to obtain. Indeed, current government reporting practices obscure from
both taxpayers and public officials how much is being spent for criminal justice and corrections. One
corrections agency which spends over $100 million a
year has not issued an annual report in over a decade.

Even when agency reports are issued, they do
not accurately reflect the true costs of operations,
for some costs are borne by other government accounts. For example, the high cost of employee benefits are in many cases not paid by the individual
agencies but are instead buried in the "miscellaneous" section of the general government accounts. In
other instances costs chargeable to a particular
agency are paid by other public agencies and are excluded from the fiscal reports of the primary agency. In New York City, Department of Correction
spending for jails during fiscal 1978 reflected no
more than 64 percent of the actual jail costs. Similarly, expenditures for state prisons in the State
Department of Correctional Services accounted for
only 77 percent of total prison costs during the
same fiscal year.

Reporting is especially inadequate at the county and municipal level, where approximately 80 percent of the criminal justice dollar in our state is
spent. A recent survey by the Ways and Means Committee of the State Assembly reported that these
"government accounts are not kept in accordance with
generally accepted standards and, with the exception
of school districts, the data are not subject to an
annual audit meeting generally accepted standards."[5]

A comprehensive portrayal of criminal justice
and corrections costs is further frustrated by the
extreme fragmentation of public spending. What is
generously called the criminal justice "system" is
in reality a crazy quilt of more than 3,000 public
agencies supported by more than 1,600 governing
units at the state, county, and municipal levels.
No single agency effectively coordinates or even

monitors spending by all these scattered agencies. For example, the State Commission of Correction reviews only partial costs of local jails and penitentiaries outside New York City. The State Division of Criminal Justice Services reports only the expenditures of federal monies in the state. The State Department of Audit and Control collects statewide fiscal data on localities but, in the words of a recent Ways and Means Committee study, "the problems inherent in dealing with so many local governments with differing fiscal years render the data obsolete by the time they are made available."[6] Department of Audit and Control reports are also too general to reveal specific criminal justice and corrections costs.

The absence of adequate fiscal monitoring and reporting is especially troublesome given current trends in public spending. The increasing cost of operating our penal institutions has risen dramatically during the past decade. This is not a simple consequence of having more criminal offenders to accommodate. The cost of the New York state prison system increased more than 200 percent between 1971 and 1979, whereas the prison population grew by only 60 percent during the same period. The operating budget of the New York City jail system has likewise grown rapidly (106 percent between 1970 and 1979) even though the average daily prisoner population has *declined*.[7]

These costs will continue to rise if current sentencing practices and recent statutory revisions which require lengthy prison terms for many offenders are not significantly changed. State prison managers are anticipating that between 5,000 and 7,000 new cells will be needed before 1983. To make room for this expanding prisoner population, the state is planning to lease New York City jails on Rikers Island and build new maximum-security prisons from the ground up. This will cost the taxpayer between $70,000 and $90,000 per cell simply for construction or purchase. If this expansion is to be financed by issuing bonds, the ultimate cost to the taxpayer will approach or even exceed $200,00 per cell. New York City is planning to build seven or eight new jails, with an estimated price tag of $400 million; the cost of financing could quadruple this figure.

This higher level of spending for corrections will not guarantee a safer community. It has yet to be established that the threat of lengthy prison sentences deters would-be offenders from committing

crimes.   Taking criminals off the streets and locking them up does restrain them from committing further crimes against the community while they are
incarcerated, but this has a relatively insignificant impact on overall rates of crime.[8]

Rather than rely more heavily upon expensive
institutions, we could make more frequent use of the
less costly alternatives that are available.   Lowering corrections costs is a particularly important
goal because New Yorkers are already among the most
highly taxed in the nation, second only to Alaskans.
Government spending for all programs has grown much
faster in New York than elsewhere in the nation, but
the taxpayers' incomes are not keeping pace.[9] Quite
simply, taxpayers are less and less able to afford
higher rates of spending by government.

Recommendations

In light of the situation described in this report, the following steps should be taken immediately:

Require All Public Criminal Justice Agencies
To Issue Comprehensive Annual Reports

Annual reports should integrate into a *single statement
all costs* incurred by the reporting agency's operations, including direct costs, costs absorbed by
other agencies (e.g., the cost of public hospital
care of prisoners), and costs billed to other government accounts (e.g., fringe benefits and retirement fund contributions).   Current agency reports do
not reflect these different costs.

Annual reports should also describe what kinds
of services were provided by the expenditure of public monies.   Moreover the *unit costs* of each of these
discrete services should be reported.   These would
include, for example, the average annual or daily
cost of incarcerating a single prisoner, the cost of
a year's probation supervision, of a completed presentence report, of a completed medical examination,
etc.   This will require improved management information systems in many agencies.   Without accurate
unit cost information, the advantages and disadvan-
tages of alternative approches cannot be effectively

evaluated.

Annual reports should reveal past trends in spending for a particular agency service. To anticipate accurately the future costs of one or another criminal justice program, it is necessary to know how these costs have changed in the past.

Establish An Agency On The State Level
To Collect, Evaluate, And Report Costs
Of Criminal Justice And Corrections At
All Levels Of Government

Even with improved agency reporting, a comprehensive accounting of corrections and criminal justice costs will continue to be frustrated by the proliferation of more than 3,000 public agencies, most of which are at the local levels of government.

An administrative unit at the state government level should be created with the power to collect fiscal data for criminal justice and corrections activities throughout the state. The unit should require all jurisdictions to follow uniform and generally accepted accounting principles. This state unit should report annually to the legislature and the public on statewide spending for criminal justice and corrections at all levels of government. Without such reporting, neither legislators nor the public can learn how monies are being spent.

The intelligent allocation of scarce public resources requires that criminal justice costs at all levels of government be visible. Without understanding what these costs are and how they are related, decision making will remain poorly coordinated. To enhance the ability of public administrators to plan effectively (and to improve reports to the taxpaying public), the proposed central state agency should report the *marginal costs* of various criminal justice services. This is the cost of servicing one more (or conversely, one fewer) persons in each of the criminal justice agencies across the state. A better understanding of fixed, variable, and marginal costs is essential if the fiscal impacts of different sentencing and criminal justice reforms are to be anticipated.

Require All Corrections Agencies To
Justify Their Budgets By Demonstrating
The Benefits Of Their Services

In most agencies financing is done through incremental budgeting; the next year's request is based on the current year's spending. This method provides little incentive to analyze program effectiveness.

State and local governments must require all public corrections agencies to adopt financing procedures which tie re-funding to ongoing evaluation of service delivery and overall effectiveness. Without such evaluations, legislators and the public have no way of knowing if monies are being wasted. Current evaluation practices are woefully inadequate.

Maximize The Use Of Alternatives
To Expensive Pretrial Detention

The high cost of pretrial detention requires the maximum use of less expensive alternatives. Significant reductions in pretrial detention costs can be made without significantly increasing the risk to the public. For example, a very high percentage of those admitted to jail ultimately have their charges dismissed, or are found guilty of offenses not deemed serious enough to warrant jail or prison sentences. Many of these should never have been jailed in the first place while they awaited disposition of their cases. Alternatives utilized successfully in other jurisdictions include:

Court Summons: New York City police are now authorized to issue an order to appear in court on an appointed day rather than taking the nondangerous offender into custody.

Release on Recognizance: The experience of New York City shows that judges can release many defendants without bail, on their own recognizance, while they await disposition of their cases.

Third Party Custody and Other Nonmonetary Assurances: Procedures should be created which allow the release of defendants to a third party, whether an individual, a community organization, or another government agency, including counseling and job placement services, and drug treatment centers. For those who have weak ties to the community but do not require expensive pretrial detention, England has successfully used bail hostels instead of jails.

Maximize The Use of Less Costly Alternatives To Prison Sentences For Convicted Offenders

Sentencing offenders to jail or prison is remarkably costly. Lawmakers and much of the general public are calling for increased use of imprisonment without recognizing that this very expensive policy has a relatively slight impact on the overall crime rate. The past decade has witnessed a rapid expansion of the state prisoner population which has not yielded a substantial reduction in crime.

Other jurisdictions have developed alternative sanctions which are less expensive and not appreciably increase the risk to the public. The alternatives currently available to sentencing judges in New York include probation, discharge, and a fine. As discussed in Chapter 4, an increased and more creative use of probation is a priority. However, if the offender is not in need of the social services and surveillance which probation at least attempts to provide, few other choices exist. Expanding the range of penalties would give sentencing judges additional low-cost alternatives, including:

Day Fine: Money penalties are often the most appropriate sanction. New York must establish a procedure to scale fines to the offender's ability to pay. Several European countries have done this, calculating the fine on the basis of the offender's daily wage. [10]

Restitution: New York State laws should be revised to allow judges to order restitution payments by offenders to the victims in all appropriate cases and not only as a condition of probation as currently required. If the offender has no financial resources, or if it is feared that demanding restitution would push the offender into further criminal activity, services instead of monetary payments could be ordered.

Community Service Orders: Sentencing judges should be empowered to order felons to perform some public service in cases where restitution to the victim is not appropriate. New York Criminal Procedure Law was recently amended to allow community service orders as a condition of probation or conditional discharge, but only for persons convicted of misdemeanors or violations.

Reduce Reliance Upon Mandatory
Prison Sentences

Between 1973 and 1978 the state prisoner population increased approximately 60 percent, partly as a consequence of legislation passed in 1973 mandating prison terms for repeat offenders and persons convicted of drug trafficking. Again, in 1978, laws were revised to extend mandatory prison sentences to a wider variety of criminal offenders. Despite a cost of many millions of dollars, there is little evidence that crime rates have been affected significantly.

As long ago as 1932 the Lewisohn Commission termed mandatory imprisonment laws a failure.[11] Four decades later, a joint study by the Bar Association of the City of New York and the Drug Abuse Council found that the so-called "Rockefeller Drug Laws" requiring mandatory life sentences for drug offenders were ineffective in deterring drug traffic and abuse.[12] More than 70 percent of those incarcerated for drug law convictions in 1979 are first offenders, many arrested for selling very small amounts.[13]

Lengthening prison sentences and mandating them for all persons convicted of broad classes of offenses is a costly attempt to control crime which reaps insignificant benefits. Lawmakers must temper their hopes with realism and abandon the effort to combat crime in this ineffective fashion. Serious consideration should be given to repealing the existing laws requiring mandatory imprisonment.

Evaluate State Takeover Of Local Services

A proposal for the state to assume local probation services has been debated for several years. Advocates argue that overall probation costs will be reduced or stabilized by centralizing fiscal control and other administrative and support services such as training, finance, planning, and research. Critics argue that centralization will decrease the efficiency of probation administration by adding another level of red tape. Moreover, wealthier counties fear that state assumption will homogenize services throughout the state.

Planners should closely evaluate the experience of centralizing probation departments and other criminal justice agencies in other states. The recent court centralization in New York State must also be analyzed in order to better understand the consequences of state assumption of previously local responsibility.

Evaluate Use Of Partial State Subsidies as Fiscal Incentives

In some jurisdictions partial state subsidies to localities have been found to be appropriate instruments for upgrading local services and achieving greater statewide coordination. Requiring localities to meet specified performance standards as a requisite to receiving state aid provides a fiscal incentive for compliance with a central plan.

The current New York law authorizing partial reimbursement for probation services requires localities to meet state minimum standards, but monitoring and compliance efforts have been haphazard. The operation of this subsidy should be carefully examined to insure that its stated goals are achieved.

Subsidies can be better designed to equalize local services without causing a reduction of services in already adequate counties. Rather than a fixed percentage ratio (as now exists for probation subsidies), the rate of reimbursement could be calculated according to localities' differing needs and ability to pay. Minnesota has successfully followed this strategy and the experience there deserves close study by New York's criminal justice planners.[14]

New York should also examine the feasibility of a Community Corrections Act which links local subsidies to the reduction of incarceration, both in state and local prisons/jails. California's probation subsidy program was designed to reduce state prisoner population by providing fiscal incentives to localities. There is some evidence that the unforeseen consequence was increased imprisonment at the local level instead of expanded use of alternatives to incarceration.[15] The lessons of this experiment should be analyzed and alternative designs developed that are better adapted to reducing incarceration in New York State without increasing the risk to the public.

SUMMARY

Enormous amounts of money are spent by government agencies for criminal justice and corrections without being adequately accounted for. Even the most basic costs of these agencies have been invisible to the public eye. New York State taxpayers must be provided with regular and accurate reports of these costs. Citizens cannot participate effectively in public policy discussions as long as this information vacuum continues.

Given the extraordinary sums of money spent to lock people up at the local and state level, it is essential that more imaginative approaches be developed to deal with crime and criminals. Unless more effective and cost-saving reforms are instituted, recurring operating costs will continue to rise sharply and we will pass on to our children's generation burdensome mortgages for expensive prison construction. Rather than lock New York State taxpayers into this cycle of spiralling costs, both private citizens and public officials must moderate their fears with foresight and create new ways of dealing with this old and demanding problem.

Notes

Introduction

1. U.S. Department of Justice, Law Enforcement Assistance Administration/National Criminal Justice Information and Statistics Service, *Prisoners in State and Federal Institutions on December 31, 1978* (Washington, D.C., undated advance report), *Census of Jails and Survey of Jail Inmates, 1978* (Washington, D.C., undated advance report), and *State and Local Probation and Parole Systems* (Washington, D.C., 1978).

2. See note 1 for 1978 data; 1972 data from *Prisoners in State and Federal Institutions on December 31, 1972* (Washington, D.C.). For an excellent analysis of historical trends in incarceration rates, see Margaret Cahalan, "Trends in Incarceration in the United States since 1880," *Crime and Delinquency,* Vol. 25, No. 1 (January, 1979), pp. 9-43.

3. *Urban Fiscal Stress: A Comparative Analysis of 66 U.S. Cities,* (1979).

4. Peter Rousmaniere, *The Way Back: Toward Accountability in America's Cities,* Council on Municipal Performance (New York City, 1979).

Chapter 1

1. See chapters 2 through 6 for a description of how all correction costs in New York State were computed.

2. This total expenditure of $2.2 billion includes three separate categories: the cost of criminal justice in New York State government, in New York City government, and in other local governments outside New York City.

Estimated expenditures for the first two categories are
developed in tables 1.1 and 1.2 in this chapter; see
notes to tables for a discussion of sources. The cost
of non-New York City local government expenditures was
estimated using a variety of extrapolations applied to
the estimated total local government expenditure for all
types of activities.

The total fiscal 1978 public expenditure for all levels of government in New York State is estimated by a re-
liable unpublished source to be $30 billion. The operat-
ing costs were estimated to be $23 billion, extrapolating
from 1972-1975 data published in the *Special Report on
Municipal Affairs by the State Comptroller* (1975), and
the *1978 Preliminary Annual Financial Report of the Comptroller, State of New York*.

The proportion of criminal justice costs to the total
local non-New York City government operating expenditure
was similarly estimated using extrapolations from data of
previous years, published in the *Special Report on Municipal Affairs by the State Comptroller* (Albany, 1976); and
the U.S. Bureau of Census/Law Enforcement Assistance Administration, *Expenditure and Employment Data for the
Criminal Justice System* (1975, 1976), U.S. Government
Printing Office (Washington, D.C., 1977, 1978); the U.S.
Bureau of Census/Law Enforcement Assistance Administration, *Trends in Expenditure and Employment Data for the
Criminal Justice System, 1971-1976,* U.S. Government
Printing Office (Washington, D.C., 1978).

3. *Expenditure and Employment Data* (1976),*op. cit.,* p. 54.
4. Michael R. Gottfredson, et. al. (eds.), *Sourcebook of
Criminal Justice Statistics,* 1977, U.S. Government Printing Office (Washington, D.C.,)1978), p. 37.
5. *Special Report on Municipal Affairs, op. cit.,* p. 294.
6, 7, 8, 9. See note 2 for estimating procedure.
10. *Expenditure and Employment Data* (1976), *op. cit.,* computed from various tables.
11. For a discussion of court financing, see State of New
York, *Report of the Administrative Board of the Judicial
Conference,* The Judicial Conference and the Office of
Court Administration (Albany, 1978).
12. For law enforcement, prosecution and government legal defense, public indigent defense, and courts: see *Expenditure and Employment Data* (1976), *op. cit.,* various tables. For estimated proportion of state to local expenditures for probation, see Chapter 4. State prisons and
parole are fully funded by state government (and some
federal government assistance) -- see chapters 2 and 3;
jails and penitentiaries are fully funded by local governments -- see chapters 5 and 6.

Chapter 2

1. New York State Department of Correctional Services, letter dated April 19, 1979.
2. Employment figures from State of New York, *Executive Budget,* for the fiscal year 1979, p. 120; prisoner population figures from New York State Department of Correctional Services, "Admissions and Released From Facilities of the Department of Correctional Services for the Calendar Years 1968-1977," (xerox).
3. Department of Correctional Services, *Annual Report, 1977,* p. 17.
4. Senator Ralph J. Marino, "Report on Felony Offenders in Prisons in New York State, Part I," undated xerox publication.
5. New York State Division of Substance Abuse Services, "Fact Sheets: Trends in Drug Abuse, 1978," p. 17.
6. Department of Correctional Services, *Annual Report, 1977,* p. 16.
7. Senator Marino, "Report on Felony Offenders," p. 8.
8. "Inmates Under Custody By Offense: August, 1978 (Preliminary Figures, partially estimated)," Department of Correctional Services, letter dated November 8, 1978.
9. "Distribution of Inmate Populations as of October 30, 1978 (Preliminary Figures)," *Ibid.*
10. Department of Correctional Services, *Annual Report, 1977,* p. 16.
11. *Ibid.,* p. 17.
12. Fringe benefits include Social Security (5.56% of personal service expenditures), health insurance (4.80%), dental insurance (0.44%), workmen's compensation (1.20%), unemployment insurance (0.61%), and firemen's benefits (0.09%). Personal service breakdowns were available only for expenditures of state government funds; during fiscal 1978 they amounted to $166,189,347 (letter from Department of Correctional Services, May 7, 1979).

    Pension contribution estimate is based on contributions made during fiscal 1977, the most recent data available. During that year contributions were made at the rate of 23.6% of personal service spending (letter from Retirement System Actuary of the New York State Employees' Retirement System/Policemen's and Firemen's Retirement System, June 28, 1978).
13. The prisoner-to-staff ratio does not explain all of the variation in cost because each of the prisons also varies in the proportion of salaries/benefits to other-than-personal-service costs. The department-wide average personal service cost is about 80%, but the ratio differs from institution to institution.

14. See, for example, estimates by Neil Singer and Virginia Wright, *Cost Analysis of Corrections Standards: Institutional-Based Programs and Parole,* Vol. II, U.S. Government Printing Office (Washington, D.C., 1976), pp. 17-21.

15. Because the ratio of personal services to nonsalary expenses varies widely from one category to another, it was deemed too risky to estimate the pension and fringe costs of each type of activity. It is probable, however, that the *relative* size of the various expenditures would change only slightly if pension and fringe costs were added. For example, security costs would represent 49% of the total expenditures rather than the 48% shown in the table.

16. State of New York, *Executive Budget,* Fiscal 1979, p. 120.

17. New York State Department of Correctional Services, tables in letter of July 19, 1978.

18. This does not include the cost of training; Training Academy expenditures are in the Administrative Overhead category.

19. Office of the State Comptroller, Division of Audits and Accounts, "Department of Correctional Services, Security Personnel Utilization, March 31, 1976: Audit Report AL-ST-31-76," (Albany, April 12, 1977).

20. *Ibid.,* p. 11.

21. Department of Correctional Services, letter dated June 5, 1978.

22. Don Cotton, "Prisons May Be Hazardous To Your Health," *International Prisoners' Aid Association Newsletter,* Vol. 29 (May-September, 1978), p. 2.

23. *Ibid.*

24. State Commission of Correction, letter dated September 27, 1978.

25. *Ibid.*

26. Telephone communication, Department of Correctional Services, March 12, 1978.

27. New York State, *Correction Law,* Sec. 48.

28. Office of the Comptroller of the State of New York, *Selected Operating Practices, State Commission of Correction,* Audit Report AL-ST-65-77, Division of Audits and Accounts, (Albany) Filed December 29, 1978.

29. *Todaro v. Ward,* 545 F. 2d 48 (2d Cir. 1977)

30. Telephone communication, Legal Aid Society, Prisoners' Rights Project, March 8, 1978.

31. *Todaro v. Ward,* 431 F. Supp. 1129 (S.D.N.Y., 1977)

32. New York State Department of Mental Health, personal communication.

33. Computed from information provided by New York State Department of Mental Health, telephone conversation.

34. New York State Department of Correctional Services, telephone communication.

35. See note 5.
36. Letter from Reality House, Inc., dated January 26, 1979.
37. *Ibid.*
38. Department of Correctional Services, *Annual Report, 1977,* p. 16.
39. Senator Marino, "Report on Felony Offenders," p. 6.
40. Austin MacCormick, "The Education of Adult Prisoners -- A Survey and a Program," The National Society of Penal Information, Inc. (New York, New York, 1931).
41. Department of Correctional Services, *Annual Report, 1977,* p. 24.
42. The New York State Department of Labor projects that construction activity will pick up during the 1978-1985 period and will grow at about the same rate as total employment. It nonetheless seems unlikely that this industry will be able to absorb many ex-offenders. The labor pool of persons with previous construction experience is quite large and these workers will benefit most from new job openings. The craft unions which dominate the industry are also not likely to admit many ex-offenders until the surplus of unemployed or subemployed construction workers is eliminated. See New York State Department of Labor, *Occupational Projections, New York State, 1974-1985,* January 1978, p. 24.
43. *Ibid.,* p. 23. In 1974, 72.2% of all employment in the state was in service-related industries. The Department of Labor forecasts that this will increase to 75.1% by 1985.
44. *Ibid.,* p. 18.
45. New York State Department of Correctional Services, letter dated June 5, 1978.
46. Statutory authorization is in New York State *Correction Law,* Article 26.
47. From speech by Department of Correctional Services Director of Temporary Release Programs, before the New York State Coalition for Criminal Justice, Albany, February 6, 1978.
48. *Ibid.*
49. See Table 2.2.
50. Department of Correctional Services, letter to Director of New York State Coalition for Criminal Justice.
51. See Lucy N. Friedman, *The Wildcat Experiment: An Early Test of Supported Work in Drug Abuse Rehabiliation,* U.S. Department of Health, Education and Welfare, National Institute on Drug Abuse, U.S. Government Printing Office, (Washington, D.C., 1978); see also Manpower Demonstration Research Corporation, *Second Annual Report on the National Supported Work Demonstration,* (New York, April, 1978).
52. See Lucy N. Friedman, *op. cit.*
53. *Sewell v. Pegelow,* 291 F. 2d 196 (4th Cir. 1961); *Fulwood v. Clemmer,* 206 F. Supp. 370 (D.D.C. 1961); *Sostre v.*

McGinnis, 334 F 2d 906 (2d Cir. 1964).

54. See, for example, the statement of purpose in the New York State Department of Correctional Services, *Equity and Justice,* Annual Report for 1976, p. 27.

55. Expenditure data from Department of Correctional Services, tables with letter dated July 19, 1978; revenue data from personal communication, Department of Correctional Services, October 4, 1978.

56. *Ibid.* (personal communication).

57. Office of the State Comptroller, Division of Audits and Accounts, "Financial and Operating Practices, Department of Correctional Services, Division of Industries, August 31, 1976, Audit Report AL-ST-56-76," (Albany, April, 1977), p. 5.

58. *Ibid.*

59. *Ibid.,* and "Department of Correctional Services, Division of Industries, Financial Management System, September 30, 1976, Audit Report AL-ST-30-77."

60. *Ibid.*

61. An interesting review of the history of this amendment is in the *Report by the New York State Advisory Committee on Prison Industries to the Commission to Investigate Prison Administration and Construction,* (Albany, February 1932), pp. 5-9. An early compendium of articles on prison labor is the American Academy of Political and Social Science's *Prison Labor,* (Philadelphia, 1913).

62. See the Study of the Economic and Rehabilitative Aspects of Prison Industry, *Analysis of Prison Industries and Recommendation for Change,* National Institute of Law Enforcement and Criminal Justice, U.S. Government Printing Office (Washington, D.C., 1978).

63. Article 220 of the *Penal Law* was revised in 1973 to increase penalties for drugs; the same bill stiffened the penalties for second felony offenders (*Penal Law,* Sections 70.06 and 70.10). Penalties for "violent felony" convictions were also scaled upwards in 1978 (*Penal Law,* Sections 70.02, 70.04, 70.05, 70.08).

64. "Admissions and Releases From Facilities of the Department of Correctional Services for the Calendar Years 1968-1977," Department of Correctional Services.

65. *Ibid.*

66. Department of Correctional Services, letter dated August 2, 1978. The department notes that the "actual cost per cell is not available due to ongoing construction and change orders in process." Nonetheless, it appears that it will be about $45,000.

67. A useful review of the problems of projecting prison populations can be found in Andrew Rutherford, et. al., *Prison Population and Policy Choices, Volume I: Preliminary Report to Congress,* National Institute of Law Enforcement and Criminal Justice, U.S. Government Printing

Office (Washington, D.C., 1977), Chapters Iv and V.

68. Department of Correctional Services, "Violent Felony Offender Law; Impact on DOCS Population from New Sentence Structure," (July 27, 1978).

69. William Cuiros, Jr., Commissioner, New York City Department of Correction, Benjamin Ward, Commissioner, New York State Department of Correctional Services, and Richard Hongisto, Executive Deputy Commissioner, Commissioner-Designate, New York State Department of Correctional Services, *City-State Plan for Rikers Island,* unpublished xerox (July 25, 1978).

70. The Joint Venture Team of the Ehrenkrantz Group and Bernard Rothzeid & Partners, *Construction Action Plan,* submitted to the New York State Department of Correctional Services, January 27, 1978.

Chapter 3

1. This refers only to those 4,469 prisoners released on original parole and does not include prisoners who were conditionally released or released a second time after being re-incarcerated for an earlier violation of parole supervision. The most recent figures which separate these three categories are in New York State Department of Correctional Services, *Annual Statistical Report - Parole Statistics, 1976,* (Advance Release), unnumbered page entitled, "Highlights -- State Release."

2. The average cost of operating the prisons during 1976 was not determined; during fiscal 1978 the average annual per capita cost was $15,050. At this rate, the additional 1,100 man-years would have cost $16.6 million. It is important to note, however, that the marginal cost of housing prisoners would have in reality been lower than the *average* annual cost. No attempt has been made in this report to determine marginal costs. It is reasonable to assume that the additional 1,100 man-years could not have been accommodated in the existing prisons and that building or acquiring a new prison would have been necessary. In this case, the marginal cost would have approached the annual average cost.

3. Available information does not allow one to determine with precision the proportion of the maximum sentence actually served. Estimates were computed from *Ibid.,* tables R-7, R-8, and miscellaneous other admission/release data obtained from the Department of Correctional Services. The assumption used here was that if parole release did not exist, all inmates would have been re-

leased at their Conditional Release dates, or two-thirds of the imposed maximum sentences.

4. This estimate is based on the average annual cost of $15,050 per prisoner-year. (See note 2.) Again, the estimated 4,000 to 5,000 additional prisoner-years could not have been absorbed into the existing prison system without having to construct new facilities.

5. Chairman, New York State Board of Parole, letter dated April 26, 1979.

6. Exact determination of the cost is difficult because parole was reorganized during the fiscal year. For part of the year, parole was paid by the Department of Correctional Services; after January 1, 1978, the accounts were transferred to the newly re-established Division of Parole. Estimated expenditures (exclusive of fringe and pension costs) for administration, parole board, institutional and field parole were provided by the Division of Parole finance officer. The estimated cost of field parole investigations was subtracted from the cost of supervision, and placed under "sentencing." Actual expenditures for field investigations were available for New York City offices. It was estimated by this finance officer that twenty field parole officers and ten clerks worked on investigations outside New York City. Average salaries of each were used to estimate the cost of this activity. Fringe and retirement fund contributions were estimated to be 28.28% of personal service costs. According to the Division of Parole, total personal service costs amounted to 84% of total parole costs, and 90% of field parole costs were personal service. From these figures the ratio of personal service to total costs was derived for all other functional categories (67.7% of total costs).

7. In his review of an earlier draft of this chapter, the chairman of the Parole Board argued that this "makes no sense whatever.... Any reference to sentencing as a Division program is a fiction created by the [Citizens' Inquiry and The Correctional Association of New York]." (Letter of April 26, 1979.) Our own point of view is closer to Professor Caleb Foote's: "Legal theory sharply distinguishes the two [parole and judicial sentencing authority], but the similarities of method and function render the distinction largely fictional. Sentencing is unavoidably the sum of both decisions and not just the first." Moreover, the fiction that parole does not perform sentencing activities "serves the purpose of limiting procedural rights before parole boards and insulating the administrative process from the impact of the 'due process revolution,' but to limit an analysis of sentencing to what goes on in courtrooms would be to play games with words." Caleb Foote, "The Sentencing Function," in

the *Annual Chief Justice Earl Warren Conference on Advocacy, Final Report, A Program for Prison Reform*, sponsored by the Roscoe Pound-American Trial Lawyers Foundation (1972), pp. 17-19.

8. The statutory authority for parole practices is given in New York State *Executive Law*, Article 12-B, Section 259--259-r, *McKinney's Supplement*, 1978.

9. Division of Parole, *Annual Statistical Report, 1977*, Table 1..

10. *Ibid.*

11. *Ibid.*, Table S-1. Although most parolees have served state prison time before release, Section 70.40 of the *Penal Law* allows conditional release for prisoners in local institutions who are serving definite sentences in excess of ninety days. Whereas state prisoners who are paroled must be supervised by the parole authorities until their judge-imposed maximum sentence is completed, all local prisoners conditionally released must serve one year under parole supervision.

12. Division of Parole, letter dated April 26, 1979.

13. Division of Parole, letter dated June 13, 1978.

14. Computed from information in "1977-1978 Estimated Expenditures," supplied by the New York State Department of Correctional Services.

15. *Annual Statistical Report, op. cit.*, Table S-2.

16. Number of field officers in letter from Division of Parole dated April 26, 1979.

17. *Annual Statistical Report, op. cit.*, Table R-8.

18. *Ibid.*

19. Division of Parole, letter dated October 25, 1978. This number excludes parolees who have absconded or have been incarcerated for violation of parole or re-arrest.

20. See New York State Division of Parole, Field Officers' Manual, Section 204.

21. *Annual Statistical Report, op. cit.*, Table D-3.

22. *Codes, Rules and Regulations of the State of New York*, Vol. 7, Correctional Services, Section 1915.10.

23. *Annual Statistical Report, op. cit.*, Table M-8.

24. For a description and cost-benefit analysis of a New York City project, see Lucy N. Friedman, *The Wildcat Experiment: An Early Test of Supported Work in Drug Abuse Rehabilitation*, U.S. Government Printing Office (Washington, D.C., 1978). The supported work model has been extended on a nationwide basis by the Manpower Demonstration Research Corp. Both Wildcat and the MDRC projects have reported short term reductions in criminal activity but this effect seems to wash out over the longer term when participants leave the program, often for unemployment and substandard "underemployment." However, this lack of long-term benefit does not obviate the point that supported work might be cost-effective for at least some

parolees while they are getting back on their feet after release from prison.

25. See, for example, California Department of Correction, Research Division, "California Prisoners, 1968: Summary Statistics of Felon Prisoners and Parolees" (Sacramento, not dated); Mueller, P.F.C., "Advanced Releases to Parole," (Research Report No. 20), California Department of Correction, (Sacramento, 1965); Jaman, D.R., Bennett, L. A., and Berechea, J.E., "Early Discharge from Parole: Policy, Practice, and Outcome," (Research Report No. 35), California Department of Correction, (Sacramento, 1974); and Holt, N., "Rational Risk-Taking: Some Alternatives to Traditional Correctional Programs," paper presented to the American Correctional Association Conference on the Parole-Corrections Project, San Antonio, Texas (1974).

26. *Executive Law,* Section 259-i(c).

27. See Citizens' Inquiry on Parole and Criminal Justice, Inc., *Prison Without Walls: Report on New York Parole,* Praeger Publishers (New York, 1975), pp. 6-9.

28. Caleb Foote, *op. cit.,* p. 23.

29. New York State, *Report of the Special Committee on the Parole Problem,* 1930, quoted in *Prison Without Walls,* p. 7.

30. Memorandum of the State Executive Department accompanying New York Laws, 1970, Chapter 475, quoted in *Prison Without Walls,* p. 7.

31. Accurate data on parole decisions are not available, but it appears that the Parole Board now establishes its minimum period of time to serve on a sentence closer to half of the court-imposed maximum, rather than at one-third of that maximum, as was the case in the early 1970s.

32. Division of Parole, letter dated April 26, 1979.

33. "An Act to amend the executive law, in relation to the state division of parole,..." introduced jointly by State Senator Ralph J. Marino and the Assembly Committee on Rules, State of New York, 1977-1978, Regular Sessions, S. 6912/A. 9015, p. 1.

34. *Ibid.*

35. See, for example, the proposed Criminal Code Reform Act of 1977, introduced by Senator John L. McClellan on behalf of himself, Senator Edward M. Kennedy, and others, 95th Congress, 1st session, S. 1437; also see *Prison Without Walls, op. cit.;* David Fogel, *We are the Living Proof...The Justice Model for Corrections,* W.H. Anderson (Cincinnati, 1975), and The Correctional Association of New York, "Report of the Special Committee on Criminal Sentencing," (New York, 1978).

36. The Executive Advisory Committee on Sentencing, *Crime and Punishment in New York,* Report to Governor Hugh L. Carey, March 1979.

37. *Prison Without Walls, op. cit.,* p. xx.

38. Staff of the Codes Committee of the New York State Assembly, *But I Was Free Born*, (Albany, New York, 1976), pp. 63-64.

39. Chapter 904, Laws of 1977.

40. This is a three-year project. The first two years were funded for a total of $347,433, and a third-year extension with an additional $73,000 has been requested.

41. *Op. cit.*

42. Tom Goldstein, "Parole Board Adopts New Guidelines," *The New York Times*, December 5, 1978, p. B-1.

43. See, for example, *Crime and Punishment in New York* and "Report of the Special Committee on Sentencing," *op. cit.*

44. For an interesting description of the political history of determinate sentencing reforms in California and elsewhere, see Stephen Gettinger, "Fixed Sentencing Becomes Law in Three States; Other Legislatures Wary," *Corrections Magazine* (September 1977). For information about how prison sentences have increased in California after passage of the reform, see Judicial Council of California/Administrative Office of the Courts, *Sentencing Practices Quarterly*, No. 5 (Quarter ending September 30, 1978).

45. For example, see Andrew Von Hirsch and Kathleen Hanrahan, *Abolish Parole?* (Summary of Report), National Institute of Law Enforcement and Criminal Justice (Washington, D.C. 1978).

Chapter 4

1. R.H. Beattie and C.K. Bridges, "Superior Court Probation and/or Jail Sample," California Department of Justice, Bureau of Criminal Statistics (Sacramento, 1970); Leslie Wilkins, "A Small Comparative Study of the Results of Probation," *British Journal of Delinquency*, Vol. 8 (1958); Home Office, Great Britain, *The Treatment of Offenders in Britain*, (London, 1964).

2. D.V. Babst and J.W. Mannerings, "Probation Versus Imprisonment for Similar Types of Offenders -- A Comparison of Subsequent Violations," *Journal of Research on Crime and Delinquency*, Vol. 2 (1965).

3. New York State Division of Criminal Justice Services, *Annual Report, 1975*, p. 122, and *New York State Felony Processing*, (January-December, 1978), p. 21.

4. Probation Figures: New York State Division of Probation, *Statistical Supplement to the 1977 Annual Report*, (Albany, 1978), p. 74; state prison: New York State Department of Correctional Services, "Admissions and Releases

from Facilities of the Department of Correctional Services for the Calendar Years 1968-1977," (xerox); parole: New York State Division of Parole, *Parole Statistics, 1977*, Table S-1 (forthcoming); New York City sentenced population: New York City Department of Correction, "Average Daily Census by Detention and Sentence: December 1977," (xerox); non-New York City jail figures: New York State Commission of Correction, "County Jails: Number of Prisoners in Custody on December 31, 1977," (xerox). Besides the nearly 55,000 adults on probation, another 9,500 juveniles placed on probation by Family Court were being supervised at the end of the year.

5. National Advisory Commission on Criminal Justice Standards and Goals, *Corrections*, U.S. Government Printing Office (Washington, D.C., 1973), p. 311.

6. *Ibid.*

7. *Statistical Supplement, op. cit.*, p. 48

8. *Ibid.*, p. 50.

9. In April 1979 the State Division of Probation issued a report estimating the statewide costs for 1979. This estimate used *budgeted* monies rather than actual expenditures, however. See "A 1979 Report on Issues Relating to the State Assumption of Local Probation Services and Current Costs for Probation Services in the State of New York," April 1979 (xerox).

10. *Ibid.*, p. 8.

11. Because separate accounts are not kept for each of the organizational units listed in Table 4.2, the Division of Probation computed these breakdowns using *total* department expenditures, and then used the distribution of personal service expenditures for professional probation officers as an estimator of how total expenditures were apportioned. Estimated fringe and pension costs were then added to these derived costs by this author. Total personal services were estimated by the Department of Probation to be $16.4 million; this author estimates the average pension and fringe rates to be 31.5% of personal services, or $5.182 million. Estimated fringe and pension costs were then distributed evenly to each expenditure category in Table 4.2 in proportion to the estimated combined personal service and other-than-personal-service costs in each category. An exact calcuation of fringe and pension costs would require knowing (1) the ratio of personal service to other-than-personal-service costs for each expenditure category; (2) the mix of different revenue sources for personal service monies in each category. This is because the benefit rates vary according to source of revenue. This information is not routinely kept in the department account books.

Unit costs are computed by dividing the cost per function by the number of completed interviews or investigations, or by *average* census of supervised probationers. This measure does not reflect the actual cost per case or per *individual* but rather the cost which would be incurred if a single person were under supervision for an entire year. In the Alternatives to Detention program, for example, over 500 youths were enrolled and discharged during the year. Had one spent an entire year in the program it would have cost $5,663/year. Although the available cost data do not distinguish between Supreme and Criminal Court expenditures, these expenditures were estimated on the basis of how professional personnel were assigned. Executive management expenditures are not included in the estimated unit costs. All program data are taken from New York City Department of Probation, "Executive Management Report," September 1978 (xerox).

12. Program data from "Executive Management Report," *op. cit.* See note 11 for cost estimates.
13. *Ibid.*
14. New York City Department of Probation, letter of August 23, 1978.
15. Director of Probation, Delaware County Probation Department, letter of July 12, 1979. Estimate employed 1979 budgeted amounts and 1978 caseload figures. The estimated unit costs were computed by determining how much time the probation officers spent on each of their various tasks.
16. New York City Department of Probation, "Executive Management Plan, Fiscal 1978," p. 3. Substantially the same goal is enunciated in the Division of Probation, *Rules and Regulations*, for example.
17. *Penal Law*, Section 65.00.
18. Arnold Hechtman, "Practice Commentaries," *McKinney's Consolidated Laws of New York*, Book 39, *Penal Law*, West Publishing Co. (St. Paul, Minn., 1975), p. 147.
19. Executive Management Report, *op. cit.*
20. This estimate is based on seven hours per day, 204 required working days per year. Days absent are not counted in this estimate.
21. Economic Development Commission, *EDC Probation Task Force Organization Report on New York City Department of Probation*, (New York City, December 15, 1977), p. 40.
22. Division of Probation, *Rules and Regulations*, Section 351.2.
23. New York City Department of Probation, personal communication.
24. *Op. cit.*, p. 40.
25. *Op. cit.*, p. 40.
26. Computed from information in New York City Department of Probation letter dated August 24, 1978.
27. *Op. cit.*, pp. 30-32.
28. *Op. cit.*, pp. 322-323.

29. Subcommittee on the Functioning of Probation, *The Role and Quality of Probation Services in New York City,* xerox (New York City, January 1973), p. 16.

30. For a thoughtful analysis of the issues, see Diana R. Gordon, *Is New York State Takeover of Probation a Good Idea?,* Community Service Society of New York (New York City, 1978).

31. *Executive Law,* Section 247 stipulates that the State Division can assume direct control of local probation departments at the request of the governing executives in the county. Only departments having less than five probation officers are eligible for this takeover.

32. See Dick Howard and Michael D. Kannensohn, *A State-Supported Local Corrections System: The Minnesota Experience,* The Council of State Governments (Lexington, Kentucky, 1977).

33. See Jack D. Foster, et. al., *State Subsidies to Local Corrections,* The Council of State Governments (Lexington, Kentucky, 1977); Robert Smith, *A Quiet Revolution,* U.S. Department of Health, Education and Welfare (Washington, D.C., 1972).

34. Project on Community Alternatives to Maximum-Security Institutionalization for Selected Offenders, *Final Report,* Institute for Public Policy Alternatives of the State University of New York (Albany, New York, 1975).

35. E.M. Lemert and F. Dill, *Offenders in the Community,* Lexington Books (Lexington, Mass., 1978).

36. R.H. Beattie and C.K. Bridges, *op. cit.*

37. Leslie Wilkins, *op. cit.*; Home Office, Great Britain, *op. cit.*

38. D.V. Babst and J.W. Mannerings, *op. cit.*

Chapter 5

1. State of New York, *1978 Comprehensive Crime Control Plan,* Division of Criminal Justice Services, (New York City, 1978), p. IV-56.

2. Chairman, New York State Commission of Correction, letter of May 2, 1979.

3. New York City Department of Correction, *Annual Statistical Report, 1977.*

4. *Ibid.*

5. Chairman, New York State Commission of Correction, letter of July 18, 1978.

6. New York State Commission of Correction, "Number of Days Prisoners Were Detained in Other Than Sentenced Status: 1977."

7. New York State Commission of Correction, "Number of Prisoners in Custody on December 31, 1977," (xerox).

8. New York City Department of Correction, "Average Monthly Census by Detention and Sentence," (xerox).

9. County data: New York State Commission of Correction, telephone conversation; New York City data: *Annual Statiscal Report, 1977, op. cit.*

10. New York State Commission of Correction, telephone conversation.

11. *United States ex. rel. Wolfish v. Levi*, 573 F. 2d 118 (2nd Cir., 1978).

12. New York State Commission of Correction, telephone conversation.

13. *Ibid.*

14. *Population Estimates and Projections, Current Population Report*, U.S. Bureau of Census (August 1977).

15. Calculated from 1977 County Annual Reports.

16. New York State Division of Criminal Justice Services, telephone conversation.

17. New York State Department of Audit and Control, *Special Report on Municipal Affairs by the State Comptroller for Local Fiscal Years Ended in 1975*, (Albany, 1976), p. 36.

18. For a review of these programs, see Jack D. Foster, et. al., *State Subsidies to Local Corrections*, The Council of State Governments (Lexington, Kentucky, 1977).

19. See, for example, National Advisory Commission on Criminal Justice Standards and Goals, *Corrections*, U.S. Government Printing Office (Washington, D.C., 1973).

20. Criminal Court of the City of New York, *Filings, Dispositions, and Sentences by Charges*, Office of Court Administration (New York City, preliminary copy); Supreme Court data from New York State Division of Criminal Justice Services, *New York State Felony Processing, 1977*.

21. *Corrections, op. cit.*, p. 98

22. Commissioner of Correction, Westchester County (personal communication).

23. Warden, Rockland County Jail (personal communication).

24. See New York State Criminal Procedure Law, Section 510.30

25. New York City Criminal Justice Agency, *Quarterly Report: Fourth Quarter, 1977*, p. 49.

26. See, for example, Martin Barr, "The Brooklyn Supreme Court Program of the Criminal Justice Agency: A Descriptive Summary and Evaluation," The New York City Criminal Justice Agency (unpublished xerox dated March, 1979).

27. A one-week survey of 514 persons arraigned on desk appearance tickets found that only three were imprisoned. New York City Criminal Justice Agency, *op. cit.*, p. 52.

28. Lee A. Daniels, "Police Seeking to Improve Innovative Bookings for Minor Offenders," *The New York Times* (April 8, 1979).

29. See, for example, *Observations on Correctional Programs and Policies in Selected European Countries*, U.S. General Accounting Office (GGD-78-52, April 10, 1978).

Chapter 6

1. Department of Correction, letter dated May 1, 1979. The housing capacity of the department has been the subject of several court decisions in the past five years. To place a limit on overcrowding, the courts have assigned a "rated" capacity to the institutions. This has reduced the number of cells, as has the closing of the Manhattan House of Detention for Men ("The Tombs"), which was found by the courts to be unconstitutionally depriving prisoners of their rights. See *Rhem v. Malcolm*, 371 F. Supp. 549 (S.D.N.Y., 1974); Aff'd 507 F. 2d 33 (2d Cir., 1974).

2. This approximates the estimated $71.87 per prisoner annual cost for fiscal 1976 by Coopers & Lybrand/National Council on Crime and Delinquency. Their figure includes debt service, however, which is excluded from our analysis for lack of sufficiently precise information. If debt service is subtracted from the Coopers & Lybrand/ NCCD estimate, the per prisoner cost is $65.10. See Coopers & Lybrand, "The Cost of Incarceration in New York City," sponsored and published by the National Council on Crime and Delinquency, (Hackensack, New Jersey, 1978).

3. William Ciuros, Jr., Benjamin Ward, Richard Hongisto, *City-State Plan for Rikers Island*, (July 25, 1978), pp. 9-10.

4. Department of Correction, *Annual Statistical Report, 1977*.

5. Department of Correction, "Executive Management Report," June 1978, p. 1.

6. New York City, *Mayor's Management Report* (Supplemental), (August 18, 1978), p. 13.

7. Department of Correction, letter dated May 1, 1979.

8. Fringe benefit rates were estimated by the New York City Office of Management and Budget and the Department of Correction (personal communication).

9. Estimated on basis of total food costs, proportion of inmates, civilians, and uniformed officers, and average daily work attendance of employees.

10. See note 8.

11. *Annual Report of the Comptroller of the City of New York for the Fiscal Year 1978*, p. 34.

12. These estimates were derived in the following fashion. Personal service costs for each functional category were estimated using the data from the 1978 Department of Cor-

rection Post Survey. The mix of uniformed and civilian employees for each category was determined using the fiscal 1978 Modified Budget. Other-than-personal-service costs were then added to each of these categories; source of these costs was the Department of Correction, Fiscal Control Division. Sixteen percent of the department's OTPS expenditures could not be distributed, nor could 3% of those expenditures by outside agencies in support of corrections. In comparison to the total cost, however, these undistributed costs were very small: 1.8% of the total $171.2 million.

In a letter of May 1, 1979 the Department of Correction objected to our use of this particular post survey, arguing that it was done by the previous administration and was not satisfactory. A new one has been ordered, which was tentatively scheduled for completion in fiscal 1980. In corrections, as in other industries, time and motion studies become tools in political battles between management and workers, and between agency executives and administrators in outside agencies who have an interest in changing the way work is done in the agency. The post survey used here is the best source of data at present; the findings of later surveys will be welcomed if they improve the ability to understand corrections costs.

13. "Executive Management Report," *op. cit.*, p. 8.
14. New York City Department of Correction, *Supplemental Budget Request*, Fiscal Year 1978-1979, p. 7.
15. Department of Correction, letter dated May 1, 1979.
16. Don Cotton, "Prisons May Be Hazardous to Your Health," *International Prisoners' Aid Association Newsletter*, Vol. 29 (May-September, 1978), p. 2.
17. For a useful history of prison health in New York City, see Louis Medvene and Carol S. Whelan, *Prison Health Care in New York City: A Historical Perspective*, Community Service Society, (New York, May 1976).
18. *Supplemental Budget Request, op. cit.*, p. 7.
19. Department of Correction, Fiscal Control Division.
20. "Executive Management Report," *op. cit.*, p. 3.
21. See note 9.
22. "Executive Management Report," *op. cit.*, p. 4.
23. "Average Daily Census," *op. cit.*
24. Of the allocated personal service costs, 72% were readily identified as being incurred by one or the other of the various institutions. The remainder was spent for various overhead functions, including transportation, court pens, Rikers Island Headquarters, the Manhattan House of Detention for Men, and the Kross Center. These costs were distributed to the various institutions in the following manner. Transportation costs were allocated according to each institution's share of all admissions and discharges during fiscal 1978. Court Costs were

allocated according to each institution's share of all
transfers to and from court buildings. For Rikers Island
Headquarters, maintenance costs were allocated according
to distribution of inmate population, excluding court
pens and prison hopsital wards; security costs were distributed according to distribution of inmates on Rikers
Island; manufacturing industry costs were distributed according to proportion of sentenced inmates on Rikers Island; and Rikers Island administrative costs were allocated by proportion to all other headquarters costs. Fifty percent of Manhattan House of Detention costs were
distributed to all institutions according to their share
of the total population, 50% to Rikers Island institutions for Manhattan cases (assuming 80% of cases in New
York City House of Detention for Men and 35% of cases in
other institutions). All Kross Center costs were allocated to the New York City House of Detention for Men.

25. In a May 1, 1979 letter responding to the analysis in
this paragraph, the department writes:

> The Department's post structures are fixed,
> that is, most uniformed personnel work in a
> limited area with relatively little range of
> movement. The number of personnel in a facil-
> ity is dictated largely by physical structure,
> as well as type of population. We do not have
> staffing ratios, except on a per facility ba-
> sis. It is not possible to compare different
> facilities unless many variables are taken
> into account.

It is certainly possible to compare the staffing costs of
different facilities, but *evaluating* those differences
requires a consideration of many different factors, as
the department notes.

26. *Annual Statistical Reports, op. cit.* (1969-1977).

27. Mitchell Zaretsky, "Report to William Ciuros, Jr., Commissioner, New York City Department of Correction, In Response to The National Council on Crime and Delinquency
Report on 'The Cost of Incarceration in New York City,'"
(presented to The Public Safety Committee of the City
Council of New York, March 1978), pp. 8-9.

28. See the Vera Institute of Justice, *Ten Year Report 1961-
1971,* (New York City, 1972), pp. 19-43, for a review of
this program's history.

29. *Annual Statistical Report, op. cit.,* (1970-1971).

30. *Annual Report of the New York Criminal Court of the City
of New York,* 1972, p. 11.

31. Vera Institute of Justice, "Early Case Assessment - An
Evaluation," (New York City, August 1977), p. 69.

32. *Ibid.,* p. 75.

33. Computed by dividing the total number of detained adult
    inmate-days per year by the total number of first admis-
    sions. Raw figures from New York City Department of
    Correction, "Statistical Tables," 1965-1978 (xerox).
34. *City-State Plan for Rikers Island, op. cit.*
35. *Rhem v. Malcolm, op. cit.*
36. Gruzen & Partners/Tessler & Panero, "Reconstruction and
    Improvements to the House of Detention for Men, Borough
    of Manhattan, Capital Project C-79," (January 1979).

Conclusion

1. See note 2, to Chapter 1, for a discussion of estimating
   procedures.
2. *Special Report on Municipal Affairs by the State Comptroller for the Fiscal Year Ended 1975*, (Albany, 1976),
   p. 28.
3. Prison admissions: Department of Correctional Services,
   "Admissions and Releases from Facilities of the Department of Correctional Services, 1977."
   Parole: Division of Parole, *Annual Statistical Report -
   1977*, Table S-1.
   Probation: Division of Probation, *Statistical Supplement
   to the 1977 Annual Report,* p. 74.
   New York City Jails: New York City Department of Correction, *Annual Statistical Report, 1977.*
   Non-New York City jails and penitentiaries: New York
   State Commission of Correction, letter from Chairman
   Stephen Chinlund dated July 18, 1978.
4. Prison census from New York State Department of Correctional Services; jail census from New York State Commission of Correction; parole census from New York State Division of Parole; New York City jail census from New York
   City Department of Correction; population information
   from New York State Economic Development Board, *1978 Of-
   ficial Population Projections for New York State Counties,*
   (Albany, 1978).
5. New York State Legislature, Assembly Ways and Means Committee, *The Ways and Means Report*, March-April, 1979,
   p. 4. For a fuller discussion of the inadequacies of local government accounting and reporting, see the New York
   State Legislature, Assembly Ways and Means Committee, *New
   York's Role in the Fiscal Affairs of Its Local Governments: New Directions for an Old Partnership*, (May 1979).
6. *The Ways and Means Report*, p. 4.
7. City of New York, *Executive Budgets*, 1970-1979. Refers
   to operating expenses only.

8. Jacqueline Cohen estimates that it would require a 260% increase in the state prisoner population to achieve a mere 10% reduction in the index crime rate. See her article, "The Incapacitative Effect of Imprisonment: A Critical Review of the Literature," in Alfred Blumstein, Jacqueline Cohen, and Daniel Nagin (eds.), *Deterrence and Incapacitation: Estimating the Effects of Criminal Sanctions on Crime Rates* (the report of the Panel on Research on Deterrent and Incapacitative Effects), National Academy of Sciences (Washington, D.C., 1978), p. 226. At 1978 rates of spending, this increase would cost $642 million per year in operating costs alone, and another $272 million to $346 million to build the additional 50,000 prison cells. Financing charges could quadruple this construction cost.

9. Between 1962 and 1976 the per capita state and local government expenditures in New York State increased from 124.3% above the national average to 152.2% above. Per capita personal income, excluding transfer payments, declined during the same period; in 1962 per capita personal income was 124.4% above the national average, but by 1976 it had slid to only 107.3% above the average. In Roy Bahl, "The Long-Term Fiscal Outlook for New York State," The Metropolitan Studies Program, The Maxwell School, Syracuse University (mimeographed, 1978), p. 16.

10. See U.S. General Accounting Office, *Observations on Correctional Programs and Policies in Selected European Countries*, April 10, 1978.

11. See State of New York, Executive Advisory Committee on Sentencing, *Crime and Punishment in New York*, (Albany, 1979), pp. 13-17, for an interesting discussion of this period.

12. *The Nation's Toughest Drug Law: Evaluating the New York Experience*, Final Report of the Joint Committee on New York Drug Law Evaluation, U.S. Government Printing Office (Washington, D.C., 1978).

13. Office of the Governor of the State of New York (personal communication).

14. See Dick Howard and Michael D. Kannensohn, *A State-Supported Local Corrections System: The Minnesota Experience*, The Council of State Governments (Lexington, Kentucky, 1977); Jack Foster, et. al., *State Subsidies to Local Corrections*, The Council of State Governments (Lexington, Kentucky, 1977).

15. See E.M. Lemert and F. Dill, *Offenders in the Community*, Lexington Books (Lexington, Massachusetts, 1978).

DATE DUE